200

RELIGIOUS NO MORE

BUILDING COMMUNITIES
OF GRACE & FREEDOM

Mark D. Baker

InterVarsity Press
Downers Grove, Illinois

InterVarsity Press
P.O. Box 1400, Downers Grove, IL 60515
World Wide Web: www.ivpress.com
E-mail: mail@ivpress.com

InterVarsity Press® is the book-publishing division of InterVarsity Christian Fellowship/USA®, a student movement active on campus at hundreds of universities, colleges and schools of nursing in the United States of America, and a member movement of the International Fellowship of Evangelical Students. For information about local and regional activities, write Public Relations Dept., InterVarsity Christian Fellowship/USA, 6400 Schroeder Rd., P.O. Box 7895, Madison, WI 53707-7895.

Scripture quotations, unless otherwise noted, are from the New Revised Standard Version of the Bible, copyright 1989 by the Division of Christian Education of the National Council of the Churches of Christ in the U.S.A., and are used by permission.

Cover photograph: Tony Stone Images

ISBN 0-8308-1592-9

Printed in the United States of America ♾

Library of Congress Cataloging-in-Publication Data

Baker, Mark D. (Mark David), 1957-
    Religious no more : building communities of grace and freedom /
Mark Baker.
        p.   cm.
    Includes bibliographical references.
    ISBN 0-8308-1592-9 (pbk. : alk. paper)
    1. Evangelicalism—Honduras. 2. Missions—Honduras.   I. Title.
BR1642.H8B35   1999
230'.04624—dc21   99-21814
                                                                                CIP

| 18 | 17 | 16 | 15 | 14 | 13 | 12 | 11 | 10 | 9 | 8 | 7 | 6 | 5 | 4 | 3 | 2 | 1 |
| 13 | 12 | 11 | 10 | 09 | 08 | 07 | 06 | 05 | 04 | 03 | 02 | 01 | 00 | 99 |

This book is dedicated to my parents,
Bruce and Marcella Baker

Contents

Acknowledgments

Several years ago a friend and I talked about writing a book together. We wanted to avoid the practice of writing alone. I hope that someday we will write a book together, but writing this book has taught me that, even though a book has only one name on the cover, it is hardly an individual's project. Many people took part in the creation of this book.

In 1983 a lecture by Doug Frank on "Religion and Faith" left me with questions on the implications of what he said for the church. This book is fruit of that lecture and evidence that I continue, in both thought and practice, to work out its implications.

While I was at New College Berkeley, Joel Green encouraged me to pursue an M.A. in biblical studies. He told me it would make me a better theologian. This book demonstrates the value of having serious biblical study at the heart of theological and ethical reflection. Joel gave me the tools to do that biblical study.

I have lived in Honduras a total of nine years. One of the richest parts of that experience has been my relationship with Amor Fe y Vida Church. This book is a direct product of questions that arose in conversation with people from that church and things we learned as we studied Galatians. The book is finished, but the conversation with and learning from Amor Fe y Vida Church continues.

I developed the central ideas in this book while working on a

Ph.D. in theology and ethics at Duke University from 1992-1996. A number of chapters in this book are revisions of parts of my dissertation. I am grateful for the opportunity to have studied at Duke and feel especially fortunate to have been able to do a dissertation that wrestled with questions born not from the pages of erudite theology books but from the concrete situation of a poor neighborhood in Tegucigalpa, Honduras. I am grateful for the encouragement and input of my dissertation committee: Geoffrey Wainwright, Richard Hays, Willie Jennings, Robert Osborn and Orin Starn.

As will be evident in the chapters on Galatians in this book, I owe a special debt to Richard Hays, from whom I have learned so much about this Pauline letter. I feel privileged to have studied with him, not just because of his scholarship in the area of Pauline writings but also for his help in connecting his work with a Tegucigalpa neighborhood. Not all New Testament scholars would share his enthusiasm for this project.

I am most deeply indebted to Frederick Herzog, who helped me turn an idea born in a barrio into a dissertation proposal. He ably guided the development of my dissertation but died before its completion. I continue to grieve his death and feel the loss of the challenge of his life and ideas. But I consider myself very fortunate to have had him walk with me through most of my time at Duke. I hope I can give as much to my students as he gave to me. Although he encouraged me in my desire to remember those at the grass roots, he pressed me to work at the highest level of scholarship.

Rodney Clapp, my editor at InterVarsity Press, offered wise advice on how to transform a narrowly focused dissertation into a book of general interest for a North American audience. I am grateful for his counsel at each step in this process. It has been a pleasure to work with him.

Sam Alvord and Doug Frank read an early draft of this book, and Ken Morris, Ross Wagner and Audrey West read significant portions. Their careful reading and insightful comments have made this book much better than it would have been. I am grateful for their input, but even more grateful for their friendship and encouragement.

When I came home after successfully defending my dissertation my daughter Julia, then six years old, said, "That's great, Daddy, but now you have to get it published." Julia and her younger sister, Christie, have encouraged me on in this task, but mostly they have contributed to this book by helping me to take breaks for other important activities—like playing with them.

My parents, Bruce and Marcella Baker, had more confidence than I did that I would have a book published someday. I am grateful for their support and encouragement over the years.

My wife, Lynn, has contributed to this book in ways too many to list, from helping me tame unwieldy sentences to giving me more time to write when deadlines loomed. More importantly, she has accompanied me and been my conversation partner, from the day we heard Doug Frank's lecture through our years of graduate study and work in Honduras. I am grateful for our love, which has grown because of and in spite of this book.

Introduction

The Saturday-afternoon sun beat down on the tin roof. I was teaching in a small church in a poor Tegucigalpa neighborhood. We were about halfway through the workshop on how to study the Bible when a woman raised her hand and asked, "My friend told me that since I cut my hair I am no longer saved. Is she right?" I felt both compassion and wonder—compassion for the woman who was fearful she had lost her salvation and wonder at how her Christian friend had come to have such warped theology.

I have lived in Honduras for nine years, and this was not the only moment that I have been distressed and discouraged by someone's distorted expression of Christianity. For instance, during a workshop I was giving in a rural town a man raised his hand and said, "I have always imagined God as sitting up in heaven writing down all of my sins so that he could punish me." He turned to the person next to him and asked, "Manuel, how do you picture God?" Manuel responded, "I imagine a stern old man with a long, gray beard and big stick ready to hit me if I do something wrong."

In a nearby town a preacher condemned a group of Christians who, besides leading Bible studies in the impoverished community, offered workshops on how to improve agricultural production and conserve the soil. The pastor told his congregation that the group's working to educate farmers shows that they had accepted the mark of the beast and are tools of the antichrist. He said that Jesus is coming very soon. True believers must separate themselves from the world in preparation for final judgment.[1]

In order to address these distortions of the gospel in the most helpful way, I have sought to understand what produced them. This effort led me not only to study Honduran history and culture but also to look anew at North American evangelicalism, the source of the gospel preached in Honduras. I asked what it was about the form of the gospel that North American missionaries like me brought to Honduras that allowed these theological distortions to flourish.

I asked this question because North American evangelicals have had and continue to have a huge influence in Honduran Protestant churches. North American evangelicals sent the first Protestant missionaries to the Spanish-speaking interior of Honduras, and the overwhelming majority of missionaries in Honduras today are evangelical. The first missionaries arrived in 1896 under the Central American Mission, founded by Cyrus I. Scofield.[2] In 1992 there were more than 260 North American missionaries working in Honduras for more than seventy different Protestant churches or organizations.[3]

The influence of North American evangelicalism in Honduras, however, is not limited to actual missionaries. Of course, originally all books, Sunday-school material, textbooks and commentaries used in Honduras were written by North Americans or Europeans. Today Christian bookstores in Honduras do sell numerous books written by Latin Americans, but they offer many more books that are translations of the most popular North American evangelical authors. Honduran Christian radio and television stations use many local resources, but also fill the airwaves with programs produced in the United States.

In an ironic way, living in Honduras led me to take a new look at the evangelical version of the gospel I grew up with, and I observed things I had not noted before. I liken my experience to automobile companies' testing their cars under all sorts of conditions. They discover weaknesses they would not otherwise see. The problems are there, but they do not come to light except under extreme circumstances. The weaknesses may affect, in subtle ways, the normal operation of the car, but the vibration, the pull, the leak or whatever, is not great enough to notice under normal conditions.

This book is an invitation to come to the "test course" with me. We will use the very loud "rattling" and strong "vibrations" we observe in some Honduran churches[4] to help us identify weaknesses and distortions in the gospel North American evangelicals have brought to Honduras. Although one may not consciously hear the rattling or feel the vibrations in a North American church, they are there. They come from the same weak points that have caused the much more noticeable rattling and vibrating in Honduran churches.

After using the test course to identify problems areas, this book will explore what has caused these "weak welds" in the gospel we live and preach in North America. We will then turn to Paul and his letter to the Galatians for help in addressing the problems.

In response to the woman's question about cutting her hair and salvation, I quickly thought of Paul's letter to the Galatians. As I studied Galatians, however, I found more than I had expected. I had envisioned using Galatians as a tool against legalism, but found that Paul does much more in Galatians than simply correct an erroneous notion about the way of individual salvation. In fact, Galatians is first and foremost a letter about Christian community.

In this book I invite you to join me in a "test drive" in Honduras to observe a number of barriers to authentic Christian community and then to reflect on aspects of North American evangelicalism that have caused the growth of these barriers both in Honduras and North America. After a careful study of Paul's letter to the Galatians, which we will read in a much less individualistic way than it is commonly interpreted in evangelical churches, I will reflect on how this reading of Galatians can help us experience the freedom Paul proclaims and experience richer and deeper community today.

1

Bound Together
in Community

LAS MESETAS, POPULATION ABOUT 13,000, IS ONE OF THE numerous upstart neighborhoods that have encircled Tegucigalpa in the last twenty years.[1] Tegucigalpa's population has more than doubled as people have flocked to the city with hopes of a better life. The hope burns as bright as the city lights that penetrate the dark night when a bus from rural Honduras rounds the bend in the mountainous highway and the lights of Tegucigalpa sparkle below. The city curving its way through the valley, over and around small hills, is beautiful at night.

Daytime reveals another reality. Dust and diesel fumes fill the air of Tegucigalpa's narrow streets, which navigate the many hills in a haphazard fashion. Buses crammed with people clog center-city streets. As they move toward the fringes, traffic lightens, but the roads get worse. Buses arriving in Las Mesetas swerve to avoid numerous potholes. The hills that had sparkled the night before offer no beauty in the light of day. The view from the bus window reveals hills piled with small shacks; many appear as if they had been tossed like dice onto the hillside. Beyond these hills others arise, ones that had been clothed in darkness at night because they have no electricity. The hills now reveal dirt roads and pathways snaking out from the city of hope, reaching the doors of more shacks. Unfortunately, the path from these one-roomed homes to the city usually proves that the hope of the city is an illusion, just as its nighttime beauty is an illusion.

Unemployment in Honduras is above thirty percent, and underemployment is much higher. Many people who live in places like Las Mesetas stand on city sidewalks selling small items such as gum, bananas or newspapers. Unlike the countryside, where even a poor piece of hilly land would yield some harvest, the city gives nothing. Many beg, borrow or steal to survive. Why do they come? Many who live in Las Mesetas are from the south where years of drought have made survival difficult. The city offers better education and health care and that often illusory hope—a job.

In 1979, when Las Mesetas began as a squatter community, it lay on the edge of the city. Now newer arrivals have filled the hills around it. It is not the worst place to live, nor is it home to the poorest people of Tegucigalpa. It boasts a large, level dirt soccer field, because the original community organizers worked to keep the area clear. Las Mesetas now has electricity, and the vast majority of the homes have had running water since 1993. Even so, health problems abound and malnutrition plagues many. Crime is high; Las Mesetas is one of the most violent neighborhoods in the city. Although most homes have outhouses, the rocky soil and hilly terrain cause some sewage to leech out and run down the dirt streets, mixing with the waste water draining from each house. Like anywhere in Honduras, alcoholism, machismo, sexual promiscuity, and abandoned mothers and children abound. A third of the people have not finished grade school.

Evangelical Churches: Why the Growth?

Similar to many places in Latin America, there are more evangelical churches in Las Mesetas than there were ten years ago.[2] The churches meet almost every night of the week in simple structures with pine benches. The sounds of choruses, prayers and sermons flow through their glassless windows. The enthusiastic singing drowns out the noises of the street and offers cathartic release from the tensions caused by the grinding oppression of poverty, alcoholic spouses, crime and disease.

Some maintain that evangelical churches have experienced tremendous growth in Latin America because the churches offer a temporary haven from the problems of the neighborhood and the solace of a better life to come in heaven.[3] Others, however, argue that evangelical churches have grown for reasons besides just offering a haven of escape. These observers point out that people who migrate to cities like Tegucigalpa often experience the crisis of living in a threatening, new environment without the support and direction they once received from their family and community leaders in their country villages. Churches often fill this void. Church members will frequently help new members find jobs and provide aid in emergencies. Obeying the churches' rules brings a sense of order to people's lives and allows them to identify themselves as part of the church community, which provides an important sense of belonging.[4]

Communities of Rules

Evangelicals are best known in Las Mesetas for their strict observance of rules such as no drinking, no dancing, no drugs and no smoking. Members are required to tithe their earnings and attend all church services—six or seven nights a week in most churches. Churches will not baptize anyone in a common-law marriage (the status of thirty-eight percent of the households in Las Mesetas). Some churches prohibit men from wearing blue jeans or shorts.[5] Most churches do not allow women to wear pants, shorts or short skirts. They also prohibit women from wearing jewelry, using makeup or cutting their hair. A number of the churches require women to wear head coverings in church.

The simple fact that church members spend a couple of hours together almost every evening facilitates friendship and creates a sense of community. Their legalism heightens this sense of community. The strict and literal conformity to a code of rules that sets evangelical Christians apart from others also brings them together. They are bound together by the common task of obeying the rules and the common experience of being different from those around them. Rules create community, by defining clearly who is "in" and who is "out."

Is this legalism a good thing? Some non-Christian sociologists and anthropologists have written positively about Latin American evangelicals' legalism. Besides offering the stability and order described above, some of the rules, especially the prohibition of alcohol, bring significant, positive changes to many families. That truly is a good thing, but I want to go beyond the questions the social scientists are asking. Does adherence to these rules improve the quality of Christian community in these churches, or does their legalism hinder them from living as authentic Christian communities?[6]

Legalism certainly helps some people to not drink, but it also forces people to live with questions and burdens like the incident I mentioned in the introduction when a woman in Las Mesetas said to me, "My friend told me that I have lost my salvation since I cut my hair." Her statement left me wondering about the nature of the communities bound together by lists of rules. To explore more deeply the nature of the communities, I took time to visit some of the evangelical churches in Las Mesetas (there are ten); I also interviewed various church members and nonevangelicals.[7] I sought to better understand how this rigorous approach to rules of behavior affected the people themselves, how it affected their relations with others and how it affected their concept of God. Join me, in the pages that follow, in walking the dirt streets of Las Mesetas and listening to people talk about these communities of rules.

Rules and the People's Concept of a Good Christian

What does one need to do to be an evangelical believer? According to a woman who goes to church occasionally, but who had gone faithfully for a year, "One must have a clean slate with God: be faithful, behave well, and obey the rules."[8]

When asked to finish the phrase: "A Christian is someone who _____," all of the church members I interviewed included the idea of putting into practice what the Bible says or following the example of Jesus. Many said nothing else.[9] Their concept of Christianity focused especially on the person's behavior. Only three church members mentioned belief in Christ or forgiveness of sins in their answer.

Although all of these people focused on behavior in defining who a Christian is, they gave a different answer when asked what one had to do to become a Christian. They gave answers that included the traditional evangelical emphasis on grace and forgiveness of sin. They said one must admit that one is a sinner and believe that through Jesus Christ there is forgiveness.

The evangelicals in Las Mesetas would argue strongly for the doctrine that a person is saved not by his or her deeds but by the grace of God. This moment of grace, however, is fleeting. When it comes to staying in the church, a person's works become the priority. As one church member stated, "The way it is here, a person accepts Christ one day and the next day the church leaders arrive with the machete to tell the person what to do and what not to do."

This emphasis on behavior defining who is and who is not a believer affects the way nonevangelicals think about evangelical Christianity. When I asked Catholics and people on the fringes of evangelicalism what one needed to do to become an evangelical, all except one spoke of behavior and obeying rules.[10] The evangelical emphasis on rules has apparently overwhelmed the doctrine of grace. Clearly, outside the church and, we will later see, inside the church as well, people think that evangelicals teach that one must be good in order to be a Christian and go to heaven.[11] Nonevangelicals tend to think they must straighten out their lives in order to become an evangelical Christian. A woman who liked to visit evangelical churches said, "I almost accepted Jesus Christ last night." When I asked why she had not, she explained she could not accept Jesus because she was a sinner. For her, accepting Jesus and complying with the rules of the church were the same thing. For various reasons she could not marry her common-law husband, and therefore, from her perspective, she could not become an evangelical Christian.[12]

If asked specifically, the members of the churches she visited, like the ones I interviewed, would probably say that putting your life in order comes *after* accepting Jesus Christ as your Savior. Yet they have communicated something quite different to this woman and others like her. Or, at least, they have not done enough to correct her mistaken view.

These rules about behavior are central to the community identity of evangelical churches. Although there is plenty of talk about God in the churches, one senses that the most important "doctrines" are the ones that deal with behavior. When I asked evangelicals how their church differed from the other churches in Las Mesetas, they usually mentioned first how the Central American Church, La Mizpa, did not clap their hands and had much mellower times of worship. Then people would say there were some doctrinal differences with other churches. When I asked for examples, they almost always mentioned "doctrines" like "The women in our church do not wear head coverings," or "We do not believe in remarriage after divorce." They equated rules to doctrine and rarely mentioned a difference between churches that actually related to doctrinal or theological belief.

Motivation to Obey the Rules

I wanted to go up front to lead the songs and preach. That motivated me to attend faithfully and obey the rules. *(a nineteen-year-old woman recalling what she thought when she was fifteen)*

Because of my studies I started to only go to church on Saturday and Sunday. No one ever came and told me that I lost my privileges, but they stopped asking me to lead any part of the church service. *(a woman who eventually left that church)*

A few church members complained that little explanation came with the rules. They wished there was more emphasis given to explaining why certain things were harmful. Church leaders had simply told them not to do certain things and usually gave a verse from the Bible to back up the command. Any explanation did not go much beyond the idea that Christians must differentiate themselves from the world.

Only baptized church members in good standing (those who keep the rules) may hold positions of leadership in the church or preach, lead singing or sing solos during a church service. Just as the prospect of obtaining these privileges motivates people to begin to comply with the rules, the threat of losing privileges deters people from breaking the rules. If they break a rule, people are placed in *disciplina* for a period of time, losing their privileges.

In the Las Mesetas evangelical churches, gaining or losing privileges are the main means of rewarding good behavior and punishing bad behavior. In addition, since many Hondurans view God as a figure who rewards good behavior and punishes bad, churches often link God's actions directly to the behavior of the individual Christians. While preaching about healing, one speaker said, "When we want to receive something from God, we must first do what God asks us to do."[13] In one church when a man stopped attending, the pastor prayed that God would cause him to lose his job to show him the error of his ways. Those listening to the prayer would have to wonder what punishment the pastor would seek if *they* left the church community.

> One time the church sent us out to evangelize. They did not train us, and I had never gone before. They paired me with a teenage boy who had some experience. I talked with the woman at the first house we went to. She said she was a Catholic and content. So I did not push her, and we left very soon. Out in the street the boy said to me, "You are nothing of a Christian if you cannot convince a Catholic. A Christian knows how to conquer someone for Christ. Let's go back and I'll show you how." I was embarrassed and felt like a failure. I've never gone evangelizing since then. (*a teenage woman who is an active church member*)

The phrase *Ella no anda bien con Dios*—literally, "She does not walk well with God"—marks failure for those aspiring to holiness. They know these words will be applied to them if they do not obey the rules. The desire to avoid shame motivates evangelicals to obey. The same shame, however, can cause church members to totally drop out of the community if they do stumble. One woman reported that to be at peace with others in the church, to feel comfortable in relation to them, one must obey the rules. As Rubem Alves writes, "The Christian is confronted with the terrible certainty that he or she will be accepted by the community only if he or she does not transgress the limits of the permissible."[14]

I had invited a friend to the Saturday night young people's church service. In the middle of his sermon, the speaker covered a glass with mud. He asked, "Can God live in such a dirty glass? Can God manifest himself through such a dirty glass? Those who use makeup are like this muddy glass." My friend was the only person in the room with makeup on. She never returned. *(a woman in her twenties recalling an incident from the church she used to attend)*

Sermons that condemn and scold are common. They serve to maintain the resolve of the faithful and to move those who do not comply to do so. For instance, preachers will say that those who do not tithe are stealing from God. Those who do not attend all the church services are dishonoring God and also run the risk of losing their faith.[15] Once again, this style of sermon plays on the fears of the people.

There were a couple years when I was pretty tense about all these rules. There were times when I wondered if I was saved. If I missed a few days of church, I'd be afraid of God. *(a man in his forties)*

Many evangelicals use the threat of hell to bring people into the church and then to keep them in line. One man, now a pastor, recalls that he stopped drinking mostly because he heard preachers say that drunks went to hell.[16]

If you obey the rules, your place in the community is secure. The successful rule keeper is given affirmation and status. There is not, however, much emotional space to fail. Because of this, it appears it is to everyone's advantage to emphasize the clearly defined rules as they do. Although the rules are certainly demanding, they are achievable and measurable. There is very little talk about character qualities, such as patience, love and unselfishness, which are harder to achieve and measure. The rules on marriage offer a good example.

> They are more concerned with what I wear than what I am like as a wife. *(a married woman referring to the leaders in her church)*

One of the questions I asked was, "What does someone need to do to become an official member of your church?" Everyone who answered that question mentioned baptism as a prerequisite. Then they added that if a person was not single he or she had to be married before being baptized. A legal marriage is a very important steppingstone, or roadblock, for many in evangelical churches.

On one hand, one could argue that this is a socially constructive rule. Non-Christian women's organizations also work to encourage people in common-law relationships to marry. Marriage gives some legal protection to women and forces men to be more responsible. Especially when combined with the church's emphasis on sexual fidelity, this rule makes a significant step toward stabilizing families in Honduras.[17] On the other hand, this rule highlights the weakness of an external rules orientation. For example, I talked with a married woman who is a baptized member of her church. Yet her husband does not live with her,[18] and she admits they have a very poor relationship. As she put it, "There is much lacking on both sides." But, according to the rules she is fine, a member in good standing.

With the focus on rules, it is too easy for people to deal only with relatively superficial issues.[19] Also, making rules the priority too easily allows the church to pronounce right or wrong without acknowledging the complexity of the situations. For instance, if a man married someone, left her without getting a divorce, had children with someone else and later became a believer, many churches would demand he leave his present family and return to his original wife. They would demand this even if he had been living with his current spouse for twenty years and even if the previous wife had also united with someone else. The man could never be baptized and become a member unless he did this. Although this may appear as an extreme example, it is not a rare situation. One man reported that he knew three people who ended up leaving churches for this exact reason.

The much more common example is when one partner, usually the woman, is a believer and wants to get married, but the other partner refuses. Theoretically, these people could be in the church for years, fulfilling every other requirement, but the church leaders would refuse them baptism, membership and participation in the Lord's Supper.[20]

This rules-mentality places people in clearly defined categories of good and evil. Most interviewees did not use the term that I am using, a "common-law" relationship. Instead they spoke of those who were married and those "living in fornication." What would it feel like to be one of those evangelical women who has been faithful to her common-law husband for many years and yet to hear someone else talk about you as a fornicator because you do not have a legal marriage document? How many women and men leave the church after a year or two, frustrated and shamed because they feel like second-class citizens?

Distinctions and Boundary Lines

Almost everyone reported that in their church people treated the members and nonmembers, and even those in discipline, similarly. They greet and talk with all people in the church in the same way, regardless of their status in the church. However, since the rules and membership privileges are so clearly delineated, inevitably, below the superficially equal treatment, divisions of status prevail. For instance, when a pastor in one church states publicly that only those who pray loudly are truly filled with the Holy Spirit, he has then set up an elite group in the church.[21]

Whether the people with privileges in the church actually feel superior is difficult to know. That some of those without privileges feel they are second-class citizens is easier to observe. One woman told me she viewed the leaders in her church as superior. She had the sense that only they would go to heaven. She felt discriminated against because only the leaders went to seminars and conferences sponsored by the denomination. She thought that unless she crossed the boundary line into this elite group she would not grow and advance as a Christian.

The lines drawn between churches, and the differing treatment and attitudes between evangelicals and nonevangelicals, are more obvious and more readily admitted. In spite of their differences, however, a general spirit of unity prevails among the evangelical churches in Las Mesetas. They cooperate in joint evangelistic campaigns, visit each others' meetings[22] and usually greet each other by saying "God bless you, sister (or brother)."[23] This, however, is not universally true. One woman stated that now that she has started wearing pants, people from other churches, specifically the one she used to attend, address her as "friend," no longer as "sister" (even though she addresses them with the terms *sister* or *brother*).

Although they claim to accept people and treat them equally, on both an internal and external level, the priority given to rules of behavior leads evangelicals to make distinctions and draw boundary lines between people and groups. Once the lines are drawn, some inevitably feel inferior and even rejected.

What Kind of Community?

In walking the streets of Las Mesetas, we have observed a number of characteristics of the nature of community in the churches. We saw graceless communities of conditional acceptance. Las Mesetas's evangelical churches state a doctrine of grace, but live out a theology of works-righteousness. Human actions are foremost on the minds of the evangelicals of Las Mesetas. They focus on behavior when defining who is a Christian and when defining differences between the churches. Naturally, by implication, they think that God's foremost concern is also individual morality, and although they make statements of God's love and grace, most live as if God's attitude and actions toward humans are dependent on how the humans behave. Stanley Slade, a missionary in El Salvador, concludes that a main reason Central American evangelicals go to church is to attempt to satisfy a strict and distant God who demands their worship. "God may be good, but He's definitely going to punish any lack of loyalty to the activities of the church."[24]

The churches are communities of fear and shame. People not only fear the angry response of an accusing God, members also keep the rules to avoid the shameful experience of feeling the accusing eyes of other Christians. Some are afraid not to go to church; others are afraid to go. One man who goes to Catholic services every week explained that he did not feel capable of being an evangelical. He said, "I am afraid that if I become an evangelical and later find I cannot do all that is demanded and go astray, I will feel bad with myself, with God and with others."

The churches are communities of exclusion. Their legalistic approach creates boundaries that bind members together and separate them from outsiders. For instance, the young evangelical women's longer dresses and lack of makeup and jewelry create identity and set them apart. The lines of separation are thick, but at a relational level, the bond of community they create is not strong. People who transgress often never return to a church. In breaking a rule, they destroyed what had included them in the community.

The legalistic lines hinder honesty and transparency. Evangelicals in Las Mesetas find it hard to express their struggles honestly for fear of what others may think of them and for fear of losing their standing in the church. The rules may bind them together, but the rules also leave them bound and gagged, unable to share things from the depths of their being. Another reason they do not connect deeply is that they begin to simply categorize people in terms of rules and lines drawn. This hinders empathy. They are not free to love or be loved at a profound level.

The superficiality of the community is not just at the interpersonal level, but also at the ethical. Although their legalism gives the appearance of requiring serious and significant change, their ethic has no corporate or social character. At the individual level it ignores many important ethical issues that cannot be codified into easily measurable rules. Under the surface many people remain in bondage to significant expressions of sin.

Legalism produces a significant degree of uniformity, but the unity of the communities lacks depth. The high priority given to a code of individual morality makes the church, most of all, a collection of people individually attempting to meet the same set of rules that are imposed in an authoritarian manner.

The legalism of these churches creates communities characterized by gracelessness, conditional acceptance, fear, lack of transparency and empathy, self-righteous line-drawing, and only superficial unity and ethical change. They are communities of bondage, ·and slavery to legalism prevents the evangelical churches of Las Mesetas from being authentic communities of Christian love.

Las Mesetas's Legalistic Communities of Bondage and Us

In the introduction, I wrote that visiting these churches in Las Mesetas would be like an automobile manufacturer observing one of its cars on a test course. We have seen things we do not see under normal "driving" conditions, that is, in the Christianity lived out in North American churches. Just as a carmaker could choose to ignore the problems that develop under extreme conditions, so we could ignore what we have seen in these chapters. We can say we have not heard this loud rattling or felt these vibrations under normal "driving conditions" in North American churches. But the problems experienced under different conditions point to problems inherent in the car, conditions that may affect the way it drives even when the vibrations are not felt. We dare not ignore the way this car performed on the Las Mesetas test course, because the "car" used by the Las Mesetas churches was imported from North America. The rattling we have heard and the vibrations we have felt in this chapter have come from our car—Christianity that missionaries brought to Honduras over the last hundred years.

One response to such a poor performance on the test course is to blame the course. In this case that might sound something like: "Well, sure, there are some minor problems with the nature of our Christian community and the way we communicate the gospel, but these Hondurans must have some special propensity toward legalism. They were probably legalistic before the missionaries arrived." That, however, is not the case. Certainly the

Honduran culture and society, like ours, has some traits that hinder authentic community, but legalism was not and is not a characteristic of the Spanish form of Roman Catholicism that took root in Honduras. As I will discuss later, Spanish Roman Catholicism led many Hondurans to view religious rites and rituals as a way of earning salvation. In the area of morality, however, the Catholic Church did not enforce a legalistic list of do's and dont's. The legalism in Honduran evangelical churches has evolved over the years, but its roots lie in North America.

Perhaps you are thinking: "Okay, the roots of the legalism in Las Mesetas do lie in North America, but the car (Christianity) that missionaries took to Honduras twenty or thirty years ago is not the same one my church is using today. Our newer model would behave differently on this test course." Granted, your church may not use the same list of rules that many evangelical churches used thirty years ago. So today's "car" looks different, but what if one crawls underneath or looks under the hood? The changes are not that great. As Philip Yancey writes: "Although the manifestations have changed, the spirit of legalism has not. Now I am more likely to encounter legalism of thought. Author friends of mine who dare to question the received doctrine of abortion or homosexuality, for example, face the same judgment today that a 'social drinking' Christian faced in the fundamentalist subculture."[25]

Yancey's book *What's So Amazing About Grace* demonstrates what I have argued in the above paragraph. At a superficial level the North American evangelicalism he describes is quite different from what we observed in Las Mesetas. Yet under the surface many of the characteristics are the same. He observes that North American evangelicals believe a theology of grace, but don't live it. They still struggle to earn God's approval. Evangelicals today still communicate a spirit of moral superiority, not by avoiding the movie theater, but by championing "family values." Sadly,

Yancey points to the same lack of profound ethical change that we observed in Las Mesetas. "Some studies show that [Christians] rent X-rated videos, divorce their spouses, and abuse their children at about the same rate as everybody else." And interestingly, he states that nonevangelicals in the United States, like nonevangelicals in Las Mesetas, "think of the church as a place to go after you have cleaned up your act, not before."[26]

Unfortunately the characteristics of the evangelical communities in Las Mesetas have more in common with North American evangelicalism than many would like to admit or are even aware of. The benefit, however, of taking our car to the test course is that it helps us see things we would not otherwise see.

Since I have evangelicals in mind as I write this book, I will continue to refer to evangelicals as I discuss Christian community. That does not mean, however, that only evangelicals struggle with the issues addressed in this book. For instance, I remember talking to a friend from a mainline church in the mid 1980s. I had just listed some of my critiques of evangelicalism, similar to those Yancey describes. My friend responded. "Things are not so different in our church. People complain about the close-minded judgmentalism of the evangelicals, but they are just as judgmental. They just use a different 'litmus test.'" He explained that people in his church would not consider you a true Christian unless, among other things, you were opposed to nuclear arms and support for the Contras in Nicaragua. He happened to agree with both those positions, but he did not agree with the way people from his church used those issues as lines to separate who was "in" and who was "out."

These last few paragraphs point to something I will address in more detail in the following chapter. Simply changing the rules will not automatically alter the nature of the communities in Las Mesetas. What then has caused the problems we have observed in this test drive in Las Mesetas?

2

Religion

Bargaining with God & Drawing Lines

RIDING HOME FROM CHURCH WHEN I WAS SIX YEARS OLD, I looked disdainfully at people mowing their lawns. I had learned that Christians did not work on Sunday. I don't recall anyone at church actually telling me that people who mowed their lawns on Sundays were reprobates, but I viewed them that way. Not only did they perform forbidden tasks on the Lord's day—they obviously had not gone to church. This provided me a clear, concrete way of labeling some people as non-Christians.

By observing those who mowed lawns on Sunday, I could draw a neat line between those who belonged to my religion and those who did not. I had the security of knowing that I was "in." My family was among those who were "right." As I grew older I continued to derive security from the lines I drew. As a teenager I felt morally superior, right, because, in contrast to those around me at school and work, I did not cheat on tests, steal on the job, drink, dance, swear, smoke or do drugs.

In college, when I met some Christians who drank occasionally and enjoyed dancing, I faced a dilemma. My definition of Christianity told me that these people could not be Christians. In other ways, though, I recognized their faith to be more mature than my own. I had to either change my definition of a Christian or refuse to accept these friends as Christians. I opted to draw new lines that would include my friends in the category of "good Christians." I returned home and challenged my parents, accusing them of legalism.

In the next seven years I continued changing. I embraced new expressions of Christian discipleship: simple lifestyle, total commitment, an openness to gifts of the Spirit and commitment to social justice. I thought I had come a long way from my high school legalism until I sat in a Bible class in 1984 and watched the professor put my life on the board.

He drew a line that angled uphill: "Many evangelical students see their life as a progression from the legalism of their youth to a more mature Christianity that stresses issues of lifestyle and justice and explores authentic Christianity. It appears they have moved forward." Then he drew a circle and wrote "legalism," "simple lifestyle," "freedom to drink" and "issues of justice" at different points. "They move along, but they are not going anywhere. They just change one means of judging themselves as superior for another."[1]

I had used the "broadening" of my faith perspective in the same way I used the legalism I was born into: to draw lines between myself and others. I considered myself right in relation to others because my Christianity now included concern for the poor, a realization that those who consumed alcohol could be Christians and a commitment to social justice and a simple lifestyle. Just as I looked down on those who had mowed their lawns on Sunday, I now looked down on those who did not share my new perspectives.

At the same time that I judged others self-righteously, I also felt looked down upon by some evangelicals for things I did or believed. For instance, although my stance on U.S. foreign policy in Central America caused some Christians to see me as a "good Christian," other Christians critiqued me. One church I attended maintained that, in regard to social issues, opposing abortion should be *the* priority for all Christians. I agreed it was an important issue, but because I put more time and energy into other causes, I felt like I did not measure up to their standard.

At times I grew tired of striving to stay on the right side of lines I had drawn myself. And when I read a new book or heard a new speaker, I often would add something else to my list of what a "true Christian" ought to be dedicating his or her time and money to. I tried to balance and carry this increasing load, but eventually it would become impossible, and I would have to come up with a rationalization that would allow me to still see myself as a "good Christian" and hope that others in my community would see me that way as well. The lines I drew damaged my relations with others and hurt me as well.

Although over the years my perspectives on what it meant to be a good Christian changed, my drive to be right, my "rage for goodness," remained constant. I had torn down one house and built another that looked so different I never realized that the foundation of the houses was the same. This foundation gave me a judgmental line-drawing spirit that prevented me from experiencing authentic Christian community in either house.

Religion

I use the term *religion* to describe this foundation that produced both my line-drawing and the legalism in Las Mesetas.

People use the word *religion* in different ways. My concern is not to argue that my definition is *the* right one, but it is important for you to understand that in this book I will use the term in a negative way.[2] By *religiosity* I mean our common human tendency to attempt through our efforts to gain security from God, the gods or something that acts as a god in our lives.[3] I am not contrasting "true religion" and "false religion." Rather I contrast religion with biblical Christianity. Since this whole book is written about Christians and Christian communities, it might be most helpful to say I am contrasting religious Christianity with authentic Christianity.

As humans we seem to have a natural tendency to attempt to reach God or enter into a higher state through our own efforts. We seek through our actions to earn something from God or to appease God's wrath. This human religious drive is reinforced by what theologian Elsa Tamez calls the world's law of merit. In day-to-day life people's worth and standing are measured by their merits. This is true in almost all aspects of life: economic, social, educational, etc. The law of merit, not the law of grace, reigns. Therefore people naturally operate according to the law of merit in relation to God and the church as well.[4]

Religion is more, however, than this drive to bargain with God through our actions. Since people often turn to God when important things are at stake, they want some assurance that their bargaining will work. Humans desire security and therefore develop systems that guide them in how to bargain with God. Of course, very few people actually sit down and develop a religious system; rather they participate in and propagate already existing religions. Most people would not, however, define their religion as a human invention. To do that would detract greatly from the security offered by the religion. Linking one's religion with God offers legitimacy to the bargaining process and to the lines drawn to separate the religious faithful from outsiders. Any group or subculture takes seriously the norms that mark the boundaries of the group. But more is at stake when one views a prohibition against lawn mowing on Sunday as a divine mandate and not just a rule a group invented. Religion's perceived link with God gives it great power in people's lives.

In some sense, religion has a force of its own. Religion is a power that transforms our human religious drive and our human religious system into a force that is greater than the sum of those two things. It is a force that humanly we cannot resist or control.[5]

Religion Compared to Biblical Christianity

Jacques Ellul, French theologian and sociologist, wrote that "religion goes up and revelation comes down."[6] These two arrows capture this contrast:

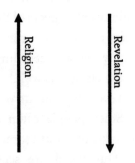

The fundamental assumption of religion is that as humans we must take the initiative and through our actions attempt to move God to action. At the heart of Christian revelation is God's gracious action. God took the initiative and came down to us. Lay theologian William Stringfellow explains:

In short, religion supposes that God is yet to be discovered;

Christianity knows that God has already come among us.
... Religion considers that God is a secret disclosed only in
the discipline and practice of religion. The news of God
embodied in Jesus Christ is that God is openly and notori-
ously active in the world. . . . The church, where faithful to
the news, is not the place where men come to seek God; on
the contrary, the church is just the place where men gather
to declare that God takes the initiative in seeking men.[7]

Unfortunately Christians are often not "faithful to the news."
Ellul states that

the really unbearable thing for us is grace. . . . It is exactly the
opposite of everything our religious sentiments are looking
for. . . . We do not want grace. . . . It does not satisfy religious
needs. . . . We are possessed by an obsessional desire to justify
ourselves, to declare that we are righteous, to be righteous in
our own eyes, to seem to be righteous in the eyes of others.
. . . Saying that God loves us grants us no reassurance. We
would prefer it if he gave us fifty things to do, so that when
we had done them we could be at peace. We do not want an
ongoing relationship with God. We prefer a rule.[8]

Because of this tension, Ellul states that Christians have always
tended to transform Christianity, something that is fundamen-
tally antireligious, into Christian religion:

They objectify it, transform a momentary illumination into
a permanent establishment, a promise into law, hope into
an institution, love into a series of works and charities, the
Holy Spirit into a jurist, and the explosion of the Word into
rituals and feasts. God's will *hic et nunc* is turned into a rigid
commandment, dialogue into the catechism, symbolic offerings into a kind of purchase, death to oneself into good

deeds, . . . grace into a system of predestination, chosenness into privileges and superiority, and the gift of salvation into damnation for others. In effect this is separating the word from the one who pronounces it.[9]

The God of Religion

As the last line of the above quote indicates, this religious subversion of Christianity goes to the core of Christian revelation because it changes the way people view God. Religion, as a human construct, imagines God as a God "ought" to be, powerful and high above us. The God of religion must be powerful so that he can offer the protection and security we crave. Humans imagine that this God angrily punishes misdeeds and demands good deeds and sacrifices before acting on our behalf. The powerful, accusing God of religion stands as a threatening authority behind the rules imposed by a religious system. With this God as enforcer, people feel extra motivation to obey the rules and stay within the lines drawn by their religion.

In Central American evangelical churches, like those in Las Mesetas, this religious conception of God has in many ways replaced the God revealed in Jesus Christ. Missionary Stan Slade observes that

[people have the attitude] that God only responds to those who pay their dues: He only takes care of those who make the sacrifice to attend all the worship services, the vigils and the fasts. . . . The brothers and sisters do not converse with a loving God who is present at every moment. They talk to a severe and distant God, one who is angry and vengeful. But, in fact, they do not "talk" with him. They cry out to him from far away, pleading and begging for his mercy. They are not at all confident that the Lord hears them—much less that the Lord loves them. Just the opposite: it is necessary to win his favor. One must merit, must "become worthy" or, at least, "buy" his blessing. Frequently, believers enter into a kind of barter, offering to pay God in kind for services rendered.[10]

Cultural and historical factors have contributed to Las Mesetas evangelicals having this concept of God, and North American evangelicalism is part of the mix.[11] Some evangelical missionaries, even if inadvertently or unknowingly, brought to Honduras "the good news of God's love . . . confusingly intermixed with the bad news of a demanding God."[12] They brought the God they had grown up with, an enforcer of religious rules wearing the garments of the Christian God of love. It was the God of the big accusing eye they had sung about in Sunday school:

Oh, be careful little hands what you do,
Oh, be careful little hands what you do,
For the Father up above is looking down in love,
Oh, be careful little hands what you do.[13]

Evangelical historian Doug Frank recalls:

As a kid, I was commanded to love God. I tried earnestly to do so. But a steady diet of Sunday-school stories and revival sermons left my young heart doubting God's love for me. I was to love a person who commanded me, under threat of eternal hell fire, to love him? Would I love the neighborhood bully if he grabbed me on the street and commanded me to love him? My only recourse was to redefine love as an act of will and redouble my willful efforts to love God.[14]

This is not everyone's experience, but it is far too common. Frank, who has done extensive research and reflection on the "strangely distant God of American evangelicals,"[15] observes that for many evangelicals

> the God who lives in their guts is a big powerful man who
> directs human affairs at a distance according to a plan.
> Holiness, defined as moral perfection, is his distinguishing
> attribute. He works hard at keeping people in line. He gets
> angry and coercive when they disobey or reject him. He
> loves, but conditionally. His character is so rigid that he
> must punish sinners eternally unless they love him for
> punishing his Son instead of them. He is a magisterial
> patriarch who ultimately fails to love his enemies.[16]

Frank laments how drastically this description differs from the
God revealed in Jesus Christ and admits that "this is not the
careful portrait of theologians. But for many of us—more, I
believe, than are aware of it—the careful portraits are in our
heads, and another God lives in our guts."[17]

We have observed that religion leads to seeing God as a distant,
accusing figure. But this is not just a one-way street. The relation
between this concept of God and people's religiosity is mutually
supportive and interactive. If people perceive God as distant,
angry and accusing, then a religious lifestyle of seeking to appease
this threatening power is a natural response. Accepting Jesus as
one's Savior, becoming a believer, can be felt as something done
to get on the good side of this threatening God, rather than an
experience of God's unconditional love.

Building on a Religious Foundation

Evangelicals are not the only ones in Latin America who have the
religious practice of bargaining with a distant God. This practice
predates the arrival of Spanish Roman Catholic missionaries.
Reflecting for a moment on one of the characteristics of their
mission will help reveal a significant weakness in the evangelical

mission in Latin America as well.

In the early stages of Spanish rule, a Bolivian priest asked a native artist to carve two statues to represent St. Peter and St. Paul. Some time later the sculptures were delivered, and the priest was quite pleased that many indigenous people demonstrated great interest and devotion to the saints. Many years later someone discovered two empty pedestals out in the woods, and it came to light that the sculptor had simply delivered two ancient idols to the priest. Today the statues are still in front of the church.[18] Are they Peter and Paul? Are they indigenous idols? Or are they a mix of both?

The Spanish often built churches and cathedrals on the foundations of pagan temples.[19] Whether to make it easier for them to construct or easier for the native American people to convert, it is an important symbol of how the Spanish built on top of the framework of indigenous religion instead of excavating more deeply and seeking to build on a new foundation. They saw and accepted the surface actions of the people, for example, that they demonstrated extreme devotion to the Virgin Mary, without evaluating sufficiently why and with what attitude the people prayed to Mary. Too often the indigenous people simply affixed a new name, Mary, to a female divinity of their religion.[20] Their devotion to Mary hardly represented a conversion to Catholicism. And now, five hundred years later, most Latin Americans, including those in Las Mesetas, have lost many outward signs of their indigenous heritage, such as language, dress and customs, but at a foundational level, vestiges of indigenous religions continue to have a huge influence on the popular Catholicism practiced by many.[21]

There are tremendous contrasts between the way North American evangelical missionaries in the twentieth century and Spanish Roman Catholic missionaries in the sixteenth century carried out their mission. In some fundamental ways, however, they are the same. They both brought about huge changes in people's 'superficial religious practices and beliefs without addressing more profound religious attitudes.[22] Just as the Spanish had placed too much confidence in physically removing an idol or a temple and replacing it with a cross or chapel, so evangelicals have placed too much confidence in removing practices, beliefs and images. The fact that one has removed the methods people previously used to bargain with God does not mean people have ceased bargaining with God.[23]

For instance, evangelical missionaries have quite successfully stopped people's practice of offering devotion and prayers to Mary and the saints. On the surface it appears the problem has been dealt with. Many Latin American evangelicals, however, still maintain the attitude that some people have more "pull" with God than others and that prayers accompanied by sacrifice are more likely to be answered. People feel more confident if the pastor, or better yet an evangelist or missionary, offers their request to God. They hope their devotion of going to church every night will cause God to respond positively to their request.[24]

These attitudes persist because missionaries failed to understand the power of religion to subvert the gospel. The Virgin Mary is important to many Latin Americans in part because they feel the need for a benevolent mediator with a stern, powerful God. Devotion to Mary and lighting candles before the saints are only symptoms of deeper problems.

A key weakness of the Christianity evangelicals brought to Latin America is that it is not sufficiently antireligious. Evangelicals tend not to confront profoundly enough the religious attitudes and practices new Christians bring with them, nor to think critically enough about how easily people's religious drive can seize hold of elements of the Christian faith and turn them into religion.

Evangelicals view the time one accepts Jesus as his or her personal Savior as the moment of entry into the Christian faith.

Unfortunately, this moment of grace, which doctrinally is anti-religious, too often functions in a religious way. People crave security, and they sense much is at stake, not just one's entrance into the church, but one's eternal salvation. Naturally, therefore, people want to make sure they have "done it right," that they are securely in. Some ministers and missionaries have responded to this desire by emphasizing certain key words one must say[25] and/or a feeling one must experience.[26] All of this foments religion because it places the emphasis on human action. The human must do the right thing to be saved. Even though evangelists believe that God is the one who saves and that a person is saved by God's grace, not by her or his actions, they further exacerbate the religious dimension of this experience by placing so much emphasis on the need for individuals to come forward to pray this prayer. "If you do not do this, you will not be saved." For many of those listening, who come with their religious tendencies, the act of receiving the gift of God's salvation ends up being understood as a work they must do.

It is not, however, just that the missionaries failed to confront the religion that was already present and lacked sensitivity to how religion could distort what they preached. The missionaries that came to places like Las Mesetas also were not sufficiently self-critical of the religion they brought with them. The problems observed in our test drive were caused not only by what was already in Honduras before the missionaries arrived but also by religious elements in the car itself.

For instance, most evangelicals would quickly label the ancient Mayan practice of human sacrifice or some Catholics' crawling great distances to a shrine on their bloodied knees as inappropriate and unnecessary ways of trying to bargain with God. Yet many of us have worried about how God will respond if we fail to do our devotions or go to church, and have sought to impress God and others by sacrificing things we value. How many of us have prayed, "God, if you will only _____, then I will _____"? Often the religious spirit behind the acts of evangelicals is not much different from that of the Mayans or the Catholic pilgrim.[27] One will naturally resist labeling a practice as religion, a human construct. That takes away the perceived effectiveness of the practice. That is, however, exactly why we must become more honest about our religiosity. This honesty is the first step toward freedom from religion.

Security in Being Right

My strongest religious tendency has not been the drive to bargain with God, but the drive to prove to God and others that I am on the right side of the line that defines who is a good Christian and who is not. Rowan Williams observes that Christians over the ages "have succumbed to that great longing to know who's in and who's out, who's all right and who's not, how we are all doing relative to one another."[28] But Christians have expressed these religious longings in different ways. The fifteenth-century Catholic found control and security through a system of merit and reward based on the idea of "achieving a surplus, a transferable stock, of good standing in the eyes of God. As for nineteenth-century English Protestantism, . . . failure—moral or financial—[was] unforgivable and pity [was] a foreign language."[29] Twentieth-century fundamentalism offers the security that comes from being right. "For the fundamentalist, the will of God is clearly ascertainable for all situations, either through the plain words of Scripture (as received in a particular but unacknowledged convention of reading) or with the aid of supernatural direct prompting."[30] Although evangelicalism has left many of fundamentalism's strict rules behind, the drive to be right still flourishes within it.

This drive to be right and feel securely "in" is the main

ingredient in the foundation of the different versions of Christianity I constructed through my life. The same drive lies underneath the legalism of the churches in Las Mesetas. Like the people in Las Mesetas, I craved security. My religious tendency led me to seek security through human effort. A religious system provided the means for defining and achieving the status of being right. Over the years I opted for different definitions of what was right, but I remained enslaved to the religious practice of self-righteously drawing lines. I was enslaved because I felt the pressure of living up to the standards I laid down and feared what others would think of me when I failed.

Religion is a barrier to authentic community. The lines I drew became high walls that created a community that "shares complicity in never speaking of what may disturb or transform us, only of what will comfort and secure."[31]

Conclusion

In the first chapter we observed that the legalism of the churches in Las Mesetas bound evangelicals together, but also acted as a barrier to deeper, more authentic community. A common, but mistaken, approach to legalism is to see the rules themselves as the problem, as the barrier to community. If that were true, then modifying, or completely changing, the rules should provide a solution. But this is not the case. In college, when I shortened my list of rules, I still self-righteously judged others. In fact, the disdain I felt for those who were on the wrong side of the lines I drew concerning a simple lifestyle was even greater than the judgmentalism I had expressed toward those who did not keep the rules of my youth. I was firmly rooted in religion; therefore, modifying the rules did not change my judgmental line-drawing.

Thinking about a particular action, like tithing, provides a concrete example that the problem is religion. In a religious community, people tithe because the obligation is imposed on them. A pastor may simply present tithing as something Christians must do. Or the pastor may imply God will withhold blessing or actually punish Christians if they do not tithe. People may feel tithing is a way to bargain with God. Individuals in the congregation may tithe out of a sense of fear and obligation but feel superior and secure for doing so. On the other hand, in an authentic community of grace, Christians recognize that tithing is an unnatural act in this world enslaved to money. But moved and enabled by the Spirit, they tithe as an act of freedom. Some might give out of gratefulness for all they have received; others may see it as a way of expressing solidarity with the community; others might not "feel" like giving at all, but still they may give because they recognize that this unnatural act is a very healthy thing to do, a way to combat slavery to mammon. In each case, their decision to tithe flows from within them.

The important issue is not what is on the surface, the rule or action itself, but what is under the surface, what the action is rooted in—religion and human effort or freedom and the Spirit. Unfortunately, as in my case, the true problem that lies under the surface remains invisible to the person or community. Returning to the car analogy, we could say the problems related to judgmental line-drawing in Las Mesetas were not caused by some exterior styling that can be easily changed. The problem is the religious drive to be right that lies in the motor of the car itself. Through our test drive, this hidden problem has come to light. Awareness of this religious element in our car is a significant step toward freedom from religion and freedom for authentic community—a community not characterized by self-righteous line-drawing, gracelessness, conditional acceptance, fear, lack of transparency, lack of empathy, and only superficial unity and ethical change. Returning to Las Mesetas for another test drive will offer further help.

3

Rejecting Counterfeit Community

ONE GROUP OF EVANGELICALS IN LAS MESETAS HAS REJECT-ed the counterfeit community provided by religious line-drawing. They left other churches and came together to form Amor Fe y Vida Church (Love, Faith and Life). Their personal histories will greatly enrich our test drive in Las Mesetas.

Jorge
In the past, Jorge,[1] although not much of a Catholic, strongly criticized evangelicals, even throwing things at open-air preachers in the town where he grew up. Then he started working in a shoemaking shop with a few evangelicals. Although he never went to their church, he did listen to them. One night he was drunk and got beat up, which left him thinking about his life and his common-law wife and their baby daughter. He then went to a Príncipe de Paz Church (Prince of Peace), liked it and, five meetings later, accepted Jesus Christ as his Savior. He stopped drinking, because in church

they said drunks would go to hell. Three years later, when he moved to Las Mesetas, he helped a pastor sent by the denomination to start a Príncipe de Paz Church in Las Mesetas.

Jorge recalls being pretty tense about all the rules. If he did not go to church every day, he felt less spiritual than others. When he missed a couple of days in a row, he became afraid of God. Hearing the pastor say things like "Those who do not tithe are thieves," sometimes left Jorge wondering whether he was saved.

Jorge remained very involved as a leader in the church. Along with some others from the church, he attended a seminar given by a Mennonite church in another part of Tegucigalpa. They had been invited by two former Príncipe de Paz pastors who had become Mennonites. This seminar, and some magazines and pamphlets they read about a holistic gospel, led a group within the church to begin to think about Christianity differently. They became disgruntled with the church's miserly behavior toward needy members. When a death occurred in one family, the church only gave the family four dollars. Another time the husband of one of the women in the church died, and the church seemed indifferent to her needs. What aroused concern and alarm in the church was not someone's physical needs, but a breach of the rules.

Jorge and a few others proposed assigning the pastor a fixed salary instead of giving him all of the tithe money. They thought this would both bring more clarity to the way finances were handled and allow the church to have some money to set up a fund to help needy people. But the pastor labeled Jorge and the others communists, and he said the church could not change because the issue in question was a policy of the national denomination. Within five months, the conflict had become so intense that a group of thirty members left the church. This group soon joined with a smaller church and formed Amor Fe y Vida Church. Jorge presently serves as the pastor.[2]

Elena

Elena was born in a rural town, but she came to Tegucigalpa and lived with relatives after her parents separated when she was eight years old. Five years later, she began living with other relatives in Las Mesetas. In the meantime, her father had become a believer. He pushed her to go to church. Once when she was eighteen and visiting him, she went. While listening to a song she decided to accept Jesus as her Savior. She began going to the Príncipe de Paz Church because it was the closest to her house. Elena changed radically. She became much less rebellious, went to church services every day and stopped wearing pants and makeup. The church approved of her behavioral change and baptized her four months later. Elena soon began leading parts of the worship service.

When she began going to night school to finish her high-school degree, Elena started to go to church only on Saturday and Sunday. She recalls:

> When I had first stopped going to church every day, I felt fine. I thought my studies were an appropriate reason not to go. Then one time when I was in church, a woman came over to me and said, "Aren't you going to go up to the altar and become reconciled with God?" I replied, "Why?" but then I realized that since I had not been coming every day this woman equated this with backsliding. From her perspective, I had a problem I needed to work out with God. Her question made me feel very bad. No one ever came and told me that I lost my privileges, but they stopped asking me to lead any part of the church service. I began to go to church less and less and got to the point that I really was out of relationship with God. Eventually I stopped going to church at all.

Elena found those from Amor Fe y Vida less judgmental of her not going to every church service, and she began to attend.

Martin

Martin was born in 1952 and lived with his maternal grandparents'
family. The family had sixteen members, half of whom were illiter-
ate. He received basic instruction in Christian doctrine in the
Catholic church. From sixth grade through ninth grade, Catholic
priests helped pay for his education because they thought he had
the aptitude to be a priest. In 1970 he abandoned that plan.

By the mid-seventies, Martin had become involved with a
progressive wing of the Catholic Church that stressed justice for
the poor. He became an activist in Catholic social movements.
Later he moved to the capital and joined popular organizations
and progressive political movements. Martin was an early resi-
dent of Las Mesetas and participated in the community council
and community organizations. The Catholic church in Las Mesetas, however, did not have an activist spirit or an emphasis on
justice. So he found little reason to go to church.

The early 1980s were difficult years in Honduras. By 1984
military death squads had killed a number of Martin's activist
friends. He felt alone and discouraged and, at times, drank
heavily. He did not feel supported by the local Catholic church,
nor did he sense they had anything to offer that would help him
in his struggles. Searching for help, Martin started going to an
evangelical church from the Central American Mission denomination. Although the pastor never spoke about justice from the
pulpit, he impressed Martin as a wise man. Martin received the
personal support he felt he needed at that time and remained
active in the church.

Martin grew disillusioned, however, by this evangelical
church's indifference to issues of social justice and became weary
of preachers continually admonishing people to follow the rules
and scolding those who did not. It bothered him that they simply
told the people the rules. The preachers never explained the

reason for a rule, nor did they explain the consequences for the individual or the society of not obeying a rule.

Martin doubts that he would have stayed in the church as many years as he did if he had not encountered some people from a Presbyterian church in Seattle who desired to cooperate with the churches in Las Mesetas.[3] They were much more open-minded than the evangelicals Martin knew in Las Mesetas. Their periodic visits encouraged him. Rather than drop out, he decided to attempt to educate evangelicals and help them become more involved in their community. He saw little progress, and eventually, out of frustration, Martin left this church. In the Amor Fe y Vida Church, he saw people with thoughts similar to his own, so he joined up with them.

Oscar

When Oscar was a child, his mother washed and ironed clothes to survive. Oscar recalls, "Every week at the Catholic church all the people would greet my mother and say 'peace,' but outside of the church they were hypocrites and unjust. They paid my mother very little." Their actions during the week made going to church intolerable, so he stopped attending when he was nine.

At thirteen Oscar left his home to come to the city to try to get a job and go to school. For a time, he lived with a relative who was married to an evangelical pastor. The pastor, however, yelled so much in the home that Oscar became disillusioned with evangelicalism as well. After this, in his words, he became more "worldly," unimpressed with either church.

For various reasons, a number of years later Oscar decided to become a believer. He thought he should do this in a church, so he went to the church closest to his house in Las Mesetas—Centro Cristiano Gracia y Poder. The very first night he went forward and publicly expressed his desire to be reconciled with God. He took his new Christianity seriously and became a member and, later, a leader in the church. Oscar recalls,

> The pastor would say, "Tomorrow there is a fast." I did not
> want to fast, but then I would think, "God might punish me
> if I don't." So I'd fast. Or I might think, "I want to be a leader;
> I'd better do this." In that church I found an oppressive
> environment, not one of understanding. I think many peo-
> ple have spiritual problems, but they keep them hidden.
> They have a terrible fear of what others would say and the
> scolding they would get. So they don't tell anyone. This
> happened to me. I did something wrong, but told no one.

After two years he and his girlfriend left the church for
basically the same reason he had left the Catholic church—
hypocrisy.

They got married but were not attending any church. Oscar
then had a special experience with God through which he came
to understand that God was more interested in him as a person
than in his following certain rules. Having greater confidence in
the love of God, Oscar was better able to admit his own weaknesses. He saw that he was not perfect but that God still loved
him. This experience gave him the desire to tell others about
God's love, but he thought he should be in a church to do so.
Again, he and his wife went to a nearby church. That little church
later united with the group that left Príncipe de Paz Church to
become Amor Fe y Vida Church.

Oscar longs to be part of an authentic Christian community.
He told me:

> I once did an experiment in the church I go to now. I was
> assigned to preach, but I did not preach in the normal way.
> I had a discussion with the people. I said, "I would like to
> belong to a church where I could feel like I was in my family.

Where if I had economic needs I could ask others for help. Where I could live honestly without having to pretend that I am perfect." People, even those who never talk in church, said, "That would be beautiful."

Amor Fe y Vida Church seeks to become the beautiful community Oscar described. For them a significant first step was recognizing that religious legalism blocked the way to experiencing loving community. They have had the courage to reject the security offered by religion and declare that, far from being authentic Christianity, it is a subversion of Christianity. They did more than just reject legalistic rules and religious line-drawing. Their histories also demonstrate that they formed a new church out of frustration with church communities that ignored the physical suffering of the people of Las Mesetas. Amor Fe y Vida Church desires to offer more than a haven of escape from the hunger, violence and oppression people experience in their neighborhood. These people left other churches because they wanted to participate in a community that preaches and lives a holistic Christianity that emphasizes not only heavenly or future-personal-salvation but also the present, physical and corporate ramifications of Christ's saving work.[4]

Although the Las Mesetas evangelical churches' legalistic line-drawing and individualistic social passivity may appear to be distinct and unrelated problems,[5] they are both expressions of religion—a North American evangelical version of religion exported to Honduras and placed on top of a Spanish Roman Catholic version of religion already there. After this further test drive in Las Mesetas, it is time we take a look at our car again.

4

Religion Produces Individualistic-Spiritualized Christianity

I SAT WITH THREE MEN STUDYING THE BIBLE IN A SMALL WOODEN house perched on the side of a hill in a dusty barrio in Tegucigalpa. We discussed Jesus' sermon on the plain in Luke 6. One of them asked, "What do you make of this 'Blessed are the poor' and 'Woe to the rich'?" Ernesto, the youngest member of the group and relatively unchurched, started talking earnestly about the poor and the rich he saw in Tegucigalpa. He tried to understand how these verses would apply to these people. Diego, who like Ernesto had grown up very poor and still lived in a poor barrio, interrupted him. He stated, "No, you see, when it says 'poor' here, it is talking about a spiritual attitude."

When I heard Diego say that, my first thought was *Why did he say that?* It makes sense that rich North Americans would try to spiritualize this text, but one would think that a person who is concretely poor would read these verses like Ernesto, understanding them to refer to materially rich and materially poor people. Diego had been going to an independent Pentecostal church for two years. Why had he spiritualized the Lukan version we were reading?[1]

One would think that, in a situation of such great poverty, Diego and the evangelicals in Las Mesetas would demonstrate concern for body and soul instead of just the soul. And one would think that in the Honduran culture, which is less individualistic than ours, Christianity would not be presented in such an individualistic fashion as it is in Las Mesetas. What is it about our car that leads it to respond in this individualistic-spiritualized way even on roads where one would expect a different response?

A Lens for Interpreting and a Model of How to Live

North American evangelicals tend to read the Bible through an individualistic and spiritualized lens. Built into this lens is the idea that future-individual-salvation of the soul is the center of Christianity. The lens causes many evangelicals to interpret all else in relation to this center.[2] At times it will bend or change more corporate- or justice-oriented aspects of the Bible into individual and spiritual terms. For instance, rather than seeing their individual salvation as part of a larger theme, like the kingdom of God, people attempt to understand the kingdom of God as a subcategory of individual salvation. They might only equate the kingdom of God with heaven or as something within the individual Christian. What cannot be brought into line with the central theme of future individual salvation is left as optional or secondary in the Christian life. As long as this lens is in place, much of the biblical holistic gospel will either be spiritualized, rejected or considered an appendix to the gospel.

As we observed in Diego, missionaries gave these lenses to

Hondurans, who now pass them on to other Hondurans. The missionaries, however, did more than just give Hondurans this individualistic-spiritualized interpretive lens; they also modeled a Christianity lived according to that interpretation of the Bible. This lens and model are two of the main causes of the individualistic and socially passive character of the Christianity we observed in Las Mesetas. Like legalistic line-drawing, this lens and model hinder an authentic community of caring and are a religious subversion of Christianity. The rest of the chapter will look at factors that have contributed to forming this lens and model.

North American Individualism

As humans construct their religious system, they naturally borrow from their culture and society. For example, many Christians today view democracy as the most Christian form of government, but centuries ago Christians praised and defended monarchies.[3] The religious form of Christianity that develops in an individualistic society will produce an individualistic understanding of Christianity. As religion borrows from the culture, it also legitimates what it borrows and in this way provides further security by offering a divine blessing of the norms of the society.

What is individualism? Dennis Hollinger describes it in this way:[4]

[First,] individualism is a view of reality in which the individual is the most basic entity and the defining principle of all existence. It is an atomistic conception of reality in which a collective has no existence apart from its constituent parts. . . . The social whole is a composite of separate individuals.[5]

Second, individualism as a value system makes the individual central and asserts the individual's primacy over the group.

Therefore an individualistic culture values freedom, privacy and autonomy. Characteristics such as self-sufficiency and individual initiative taking, are encouraged more than they would be in a tribal society.[6]

[Third], as a social philosophy individualism stresses personal morality over social ethics, individual transformation as the key to social change, laissez-faire economics, and a politics extolling the freedom of the individual and a limited state.[7]

Individualism is so familiar and natural to North Americans that many find it hard to conceive of a nonindividualistic society. As sociologist Stephen Hart observes: "Ours is probably the most individualistic nation the world has ever known. Our individualism is not only a set of value preferences sacralizing individual freedom, but also a cognitive framework blinding us to the supra-individual aspect of human life."[8] But individualism is not the only option. In some cultures the individual does not take precedence over the group. A collectivist society focuses on achieving the collective goal of the common good, rather than creating a situation where individuals can freely fulfill their personal desires with little concern for the common good.[9] While in an area of Guatemala where the K'ekchi', a people of Mayan descent, live, I observed numerous examples of the contrast between our individualism and their communal culture. For instance, in their villages no one started wearing shoes until everyone could afford to do so.

The point here is not to champion the collectivist approach as *the* right one.[10] One can see evidence of the fallen nature of society in the K'ekchi' culture as one can in our society. I mention the collective approach to emphasize that there are frameworks other than individualism that people use to shape the way they live. Individualism is not the only option, and we would do well to take a critical look at it.

Individualistic Christianity: What's the Problem?

To describe individualism, and even to see that other options exist, is one thing; to think that individualism is a problem is something else. I began to think more critically of individualism when I saw how my individualistic lens distorted the way I read the Bible.

In 1992 I sat in a New Testament ethics class. The professor, Richard Hays, asked us to turn to 2 Corinthians 3. He read verses 2-3 with the following emphasis:

> You yourselves [plural] are our letter [singular], written on our hearts, to be known and read by all; and you show that you [plural] are a letter [singular] of Christ. (2 Cor 3:2-3)

In that instant I saw the passage differently than I had ever seen it before. Previously when I had heard these verses, I had thought of myself as being a letter of Christ and the church member sitting next to me as another letter. That is not, however, what the text says. Paul did not see the church in Corinth as a collection of letters of Christ; the community gathered together was one letter. My individualistic lens distorted the way I had read the verses. The lens actually caused me to see and understand the words of the Bible differently than they were written.

Professor Hays then asked us to turn to Romans 12, and he showed us another verse where Paul clearly writes in a corporate sense, but we usually read it in an individual sense:

> I appeal to you therefore, brothers and sisters, by the mercies of God, to present your bodies [plural] as a living sacrifice [singular], holy and acceptable to God. (Rom 12:1)

I had always "seen" this verse as saying that each individual Christian must offer his or her body as a living sacrifice, but that is not what the text says. Again my individualistic lens did not just color the way I read the text; it actually caused me to see the text differently than it is written.[11] The above two texts are clearly written as plural/corporate, but I had read them as singular/individual.

Paul writes to the Philippians:

Being confident of this, that he who began a good work in you will carry it on to completion until the day of Christ Jesus. (Phil 1:6 NIV)

This verse is commonly applied to the individual—Christ is doing a good work in your individual life; but the "in you" can also be interpreted corporately—Christ is doing a good work in your Christian community. In fact, the New Revised Standard Version translates it as "who began a good work among you" to help us read it in a corporate fashion. If we read this verse in Greek, or another language like Spanish, it would be evident to us that the "you" in this verse is plural. Perhaps if we read the verse in one of those languages then we would not interpret the verse individualistically. At this point, however, my purpose is not so much to argue for a different reading, but to point out how most of us tend to automatically interpret the "in you" individualistically when it could just as easily be interpreted corporately.

Looking at these verses has demonstrated that the Bible has less individualism and more emphasis on community than an individualistic lens allows North Americans to see.

Individualism and Community

Individualism does not produce a society of hermits. People still form communities. But what is the character of this community?

It is a community where the individual takes precedence over the group. As theologian C. Norman Kraus observes, "Community is seen as a contractual association of independent individuals. . . . The group has become for us a collection of individuals created *by* individuals *for* their own individual advantages."[12] Rather than seeing the church as a community that offers an alternative culture, its function is often seen as only offering care for individual souls.

An individualistic Christian religion produces a community that matches an individualistic reading of Romans 12 and 2 Corinthians 3. Christians understand and experience community more as something that will help individual Christians be living sacrifices and high-quality letters of Christ. This contrasts with Paul's image of individuals joined together in one body (Rom 12:4-8) as a corporate living sacrifice becoming one united letter of Christ.

The Individual in the Bible
To critique individualism and the individualistic religion present in evangelical churches is not to say that individual salvation and the individual's role in the church are unimportant. Jesus demonstrated an intense concern for individuals. Paul's body metaphor champions corporate unity, but does not ignore the distinctness of individuals. The members of the body offer unique and important contributions to the community. Kraus observes, "The sin of humankind is not the assertion of individuality in community, but the assertion of individual self-sufficiency and independence from God and fellow humans."[13] In contrast, the biblical concept of authentic personhood is for people to "seek the fulfillment of their personal potential in interdependence and the sharing of concern for each other."[14]

This concept of personhood and God's loving concern for

individuals is not a toned-down form of individualism. It is qualitatively different. Individualism sees the "true self" as what is at the core of one's being, independent of others. Rodney Clapp likens it to thinking "we get at our 'true self' by peeling away social ties like the skin of an onion."[15] This notion is unique to our modern individualistic cultures. Wayne Booth points out that all previous cultures, including those of the biblical authors, did not conceive of persons as " 'individuals' at all but overlapping members one of another. Anyone in those cultures thinking words like 'I' and 'mine' thought them as inescapably loaded with plurality: 'I' could not even think of 'my' self as separated from my multiple affiliations: my family, my tribe, my city-state, my feudal domain, my people."[16] In contrast to individualism, God lovingly invites us to experience our authentic personhood, not by peeling away layers of interconnection and interdependence, but by embracing them.

My critique of the individualistic character of evangelicalism might lead some to think I would propose that we talk less about individual salvation. But the solution is not less emphasis on individual salvation, but to change our concept of individual salvation. Kraus states that many Christians define salvation almost exclusively in terms of a private, inward, even mystical experience with God. In contrast the Bible describes salvation as humans finding "their self-identity as *persons-in-covenant community*."[17]

Individualistic Christianity, a modern human construct, is actually a subversion of Christianity. It hinders us from experiencing the abundant life of authentic community that God intends for us.

Overly Spiritualized Christianity

Besides individualism, the religious version of Christianity that was exported to Honduras contained an interesting mix of Enlightenment liberalism, Constantinianism and a Greek philosophical concept of the soul that leads many to understand their faith as a private personal matter disconnected from most of what goes on in the public sphere.[18] This contributes to the overly spiritualized lens and model that have led to the social passivity seen in Las Mesetas.

None of the above is unique to our "car"—evangelicalism. But additional factors caused fundamentalist missionaries, and later their descendants—evangelical missionaries—to model an even more spiritualized form of Christianity than seen in other Christian churches.[19] One of the main reasons for this is what some call the "Great Reversal," or the dramatic drop in social action by fundamentalists in the early part of the twentieth century.

The precursors of the fundamentalists, whom I'll call nineteenth-century evangelicals, demonstrated significant social concern. Many evangelical churches started rescue missions and relief programs; worked among immigrants; sought or provided jobs for poor people; and provided athletic, literary and benevolent services in poor communities.[20] Many evangelicals were also political activists. Before the Civil War, evangelicals helped lead the abolitionist movement. Later many evangelicals turned their attention to the prohibition cause. They viewed it as the most effective way of attacking urban problems at their root.

This changed, however, from about 1900 to 1930. There was a "Great Reversal." Fundamentalists shifted away from political activism and even became much less involved in works of charity. Evangelist and pastor A. C. Dixon, who edited *The Fundamentals,* offers a good example. At the beginning of the century, his church administered an endowment of a million dollars. The interest from the endowment supported social service in the parish. At first Dixon supported this, but after three years he noted that soul-winning did not follow body healing. He decided to "dis-

pense with the whole business and get back to first principles."[21]
David Moberg offers further examples:

> Nazarene leaders who had been strongly sympathetic to the
> labor movement became antipathetic toward it after World
> War I. . . . When pronouncements were made on social
> issues, they were buried in committee reports dealing with
> church members' standards of personal behavior. Deacon-
> esses declined in numbers and influence, and prohibition-
> ism was reinterpreted in terms of personal salvation rather
> than social regeneration. . . . The intense interest in social
> service on the part of early Christian and Missionary Alli-
> ance members was soon subtly opposed by its founder.[22]

At issue then is not just that the missionaries who worked in
Honduras came from churches that gave little attention to structural approaches of combating poverty and injustices, but that
they came from churches that gave little attention to responding
to poverty in any physical way.[23]

Scholars have suggested a variety of causes for the "Great
Reversal."[24] The following are generally recognized as most significant. First, the "Great Reversal" is linked to the shift by the
vast majority of evangelicals/fundamentalists from a postmillen-
nial eschatology to premillennialism.[25] The world, in the words
of D. L. Moody, was a wrecked vessel. The important thing was
to do evangelism and get as many people as possible into life-
boats. This eschatology provided little motivation for addressing
injustices on the sinking ship. Moody compared social work to
"polishing the brass on a sinking ship."[26] "Some went so far as to
argue that the efforts at amelioration of human suffering would
only delay the 'blessed hope' of Christ's return."[27]

Second, the "Great Reversal" was part of the fundamentalist
reaction against liberal theology.[28] The social gospel was ex-

pounded by liberals, some of whom specifically contrasted their social views with individualistic soul-saving evangelism. In response, fundamentalists began to react against anything that even looked like the social gospel. Fundamentalists de-emphasized social action not only to avoid the appearance of having liberal theology, but also to champion the message of eternal salvation through trust in Christ's atoning work—a message they saw threatened by the social gospel. They feared that any emphasis on social concern could too easily detract from, or undercut, their efforts to protect the gospel in the face of liberalism. This means that many of the first missionaries who came to Honduras would not just have had an indifference to linking social concern and the gospel; some would have intentionally avoided doing so.[29] They brought the fervor that flowed out of the fundamentalist-liberal debate to the task of emphasizing the salvation of individual souls.[30]

The Lens and Model Produced by Individualism and the Great Reversal

Just as verses we looked at earlier displayed the individualizing power of our interpretive lenses, a common translation and interpretation of 2 Corinthians 5:17 portrays the combined individualistic and spiritualized nature of this lens. "Therefore, if anyone is in Christ, he is a new creation; the old has gone, the new has come!" (2 Cor 5:17 NIV).[31] Christians use this verse to explain what happens when a person experiences salvation. The saved person is a "new creation" who acts differently. This person has left behind old moral behavior and now practices a new morality.

This translation and interpretation is not necessarily the most obvious or the best. A literal translation of the verse is: "So as if anyone in Christ, a new creation; the old things passed away, behold they have become new."[32] The translator must decide what verbs to add and how to interpret "new creation." Although the New English Bible and more recently the New Century Version and New Revised Standard Version have decided to interpret *creation* in a broader sense—"there is a new creation," rather than, "he is a new creation"—most other translations interpret creation in an individualistic sense.[33] Whereas the former leads the reader to look out and conceive of Christ's work in a broad way, the latter leads the reader to look inward. As New Testament scholar Joel Green explains, in this verse

> Paul is not talking of an individual's renovation as a forgiven sinner. . . . By reading this text with eyes focused on the individual believer, then, we miss the cosmic dimensions of Paul's proclamation; we center our understanding of salvation on the changes in the individual believer; and we fail to come to terms with the larger scope of God's creative work in the world.[34]

The broader or less individualistic interpretation does not rule out significant changes occurring in individuals' lives, but it points to much more. The individualistic-spiritualized reading, however, does rule out broader implications and limit the impact of the gospel to the individual.

A combination of North American individualism and the "Great Reversal" produced evangelicals with the following four characteristics.[35] First, for them the important spiritual unit was the individual.[36] Whereas Christians had previously seen the church as God's primary agent of activity in human history, it now had become a voluntary association functioning to gain new converts and to aid the individual Christian in spiritual growth.[37] Second, they understood salvation solely in spiritual terms. Third, their ethical focus was on individual morality.[38] Fourth, their strategy for changing society was to evangelize individuals. Changed individuals would lead to a changed society.[39] Most

North American missionaries who came to Honduras taught and modeled a truncated gospel that was overly focused on individual morality and the future-individual-salvation of the soul. Like the legalistic line-drawing we observed earlier, all of these characteristics are religious distortions of Christianity—religious in the sense that they are human constructs that grew out of the society of the day rather than from the revealed Word of God. These characteristics not only formed an interpretive lens and model, evangelicals also transformed them into a package of beliefs.

Packaged Christianity

Religion, besides absorbing and legitimizing the values of a culture and providing the security of knowing clearly that one is "in," also provides the security of clear-cut beliefs. Humans do not like ambiguity, therefore, as a human construct, religion offers a package of information that removes doubt and ambiguity.

The content contained in the package brought to Honduras by evangelical missionaries portrayed Christianity as primarily an individual and spiritual activity. Although the package would have contained what were considered the fundamentals of the faith and a few doctrines that would distinguish one denomination or tradition from another, the core piece of truth in the package was how one could obtain salvation—forgiveness for sins and eternal life. This very often was literally a formularized and packaged version that would fit in a small tract such as "The Four Spiritual Laws" or "Steps to Peace with God." As we have seen, in the area of morality the package contained a list of actions forbidden to Christians and a list of things that Christians should do. The sins listed were easily definable individual acts.

Latin American missiologist Samuel Escobar described this same phenomenon when he critiqued the practice of reducing the richness of the biblical message to four "laws," five "principles," or ten "rules." . . . In the evangelical world those who believe that the answer to the question, "What is the gospel?" is simple, generally try to force upon us a simple answer elaborated by someone in Texas or California that only needs to be translated and distributed efficiently according to marketing principles.[40]

As Escobar's quote implies, the problem is not just the content, but the attitude that one could carry this package to any place or any culture. The missionary only has to translate it from English to the native language. Behind this lies the assumption that the propositions assembled in this package represent the definitive truth of Christianity as it has been and will be for all time.[41] Ironically, far from being truths extracted directly from the Bible, many of the truths within the package are more a product of the individualistic-spiritualized setting of the North American evangelicals who constructed and delivered the package.[42]

Since the missionary could simply take the truths out of the package and communicate them with no need to reflect on contextual issues in relation to the gospel, there was no need to do theology in the context of Las Mesetas. The theology had been done; one simply had to communicate it. So, as René Padilla observes, in a number of theological institutions in Latin America the curriculum is a photocopy of the curriculum used at similar institutions in the United States.[43] In Las Mesetas I encountered a simple but graphic example of packaged Christianity and its lack of attention to context. A woman told me that people from her church could not participate in the local community council because they could not be in *logias*. That was a new Spanish word for me. When I asked her to explain, it became evident that she was not sure what the word *logias* meant either. She showed me, however, a pamphlet called "29 Important Biblical Truths." The tract came from the denomination's U.S. headquarters and was a translation of the English version.[44] When I looked in a Spanish/English dictionary I discovered that in reality, what the church in its U.S. context had prohibited was membership in lodges and secret societies. Apparently, since these were unknown in Las Mesetas, someone applied the rule to the community council.

René Padilla points out that a byproduct of this lack of attention to contextual issues is that "in many parts of the world Christianity is regarded as an ethnic religion, the white man's religion. The gospel has a foreign sound, or no sound at all, in relation to many of the dreams and anxieties, problems and questions, values and customs of people."[45]

Even if people from another culture accept Christianity, its packaged form discourages them from seeking to relate the gospel in any profound way to the specific situation around them. Instead, having the gospel in a package communicates the notion that the gospel is above or independent of culture. That reinforces a spiritualized Christianity. Christianity is either floating above the culture or buried within the individual soul.

Plutarco Bonilla describes this packaged Christianity as fossilized.[46] This form discourages Hondurans from thinking critically about the gospel brought from the North, just as it discourages North Americans from doing the same. Our test drive in Las Mesetas calls us to evaluate the interpretive lens and gospel package found within our car. They are religious elements that stand as barriers to more profound Christian community.

Conclusion

For years I read the Bible through an individualistic-spiritualized lens and lived a socially passive Christianity that focused on individual morality and future-personal-salvation. I evangelized with packaged versions of the gospel. I conceived of Christian community from the perspective of individualism and hence failed to experience the richness of interdependence and full personhood through being a person-in-covenant community.

I lived what this chapter describes, yet I was totally unaware of the religious elements that caused me to live this way. I did not know there had been a "Great Reversal"; I was not self-consciously individualistic; I did not hesitate to package the gospel. Cultural and historical forces had subverted the Christianity I lived, but I did not know it. From my perspective I was experiencing authentic Christian community and interpreting the Bible just the same as Paul himself would have. I was in the grasp of religion, yet just as with my religious line-drawing, I was unaware of religion's power on me. And as I noted in relation to religious line-drawing, awareness and honesty about the religious distortion are important steps toward freedom from religion.

I have brought you on a "test drive" in Honduras because living here began to open my eyes to the issues described in this chapter. My "test drive" continues. I still observe and learn. Just a few weeks ago I taught a short course to leaders from churches among the Wounaan, a Native American people, in the jungle of Panama. Their culture is much less individualistic than even the people I normally teach in Honduras. Because of the isolation of their villages, the individualizing force of the global market has had less of an impact on the collectivist character of their indigenous culture.

One afternoon I observed one student carefully copying into his notebook the contents of an evangelistic tract he had borrowed from another student. The tract, a gospel package "exported" from North America, focused on the future-individual-salvation of the soul. The religious distortions of Christianity described in this chapter continue to influence the character of Christian communities—in Panama, in Honduras and in North America.

5

The Traditional
Reading of Galatians

Is It Antireligious?

THE TEST DRIVE IN LAS MESETAS HAS HELPED US IDENTIFY how religious elements have permeated evangelicalism and how these elements subvert biblical Christianity and act as barriers to authentic Christian community. Religion, then, can be pictured as a thick-walled building, offering a sort of security yet fostering a kind of isolation.

The world is a difficult and fearful place to live. The shifting sands under our feet do not offer a secure place to stand. The storms of life batter us. Religion's clear guidelines and packaged explanations remove doubt, and religion absorbs and legitimizes society's values, much the same way as a building's thick pillars and heavy beams give the building its solid appearance and hence an aura of security. Clear religious definitions of who is in and who is out are like thick walls that promise safety and comfort for those inside. This building, religion, is not a small structure quickly thrown up by a few people. It is large and, therefore, facilitates community; many people can fit inside.

A careful inspection and evaluation of this building, however, reveals disturbing realities. True, the building of religion brings people together, but what kind of community does it foster? The pillars, beams and internal walls—constructed out of things like legalism, individualism and spiritualized teaching—make communication, connection and caring difficult. The outside walls of exclusion—based on rules and correct beliefs—cause people inside to feel fear and shame. These external walls, which control entrance into the building, provide the security of knowing one is "in," but they also produce graceless communities of conditional acceptance. Together, the internal and external walls foster a community of relational and ethical superficiality. This religious building leaves people cooped up, subdivided into lonely cells by massive walls.

These walls that hinder a caring community of love do not even offer the great security they appear to provide. Although religion claims that it has a divine foundation—solid rock—it is actually a human construction. The security the building offers is an illusion because the thick pillars stand on a weak, unsubstantial foundation.

Community Under a Tent

Having looked at the ways many Christians construct religious "buildings," turning anew to Scripture will show if this is what God intended. Paul in Galatians invites us to come out of our religious buildings and construct a structure that produces a distinctly different community. The construction site Paul brings us to is still in this world with all its fears and difficulties. The ground at the site may appear loose and unstable, but Paul promises that it will provide a solid foundation for our building.

There is rock, invisible to us, under the surface. Since the foundation is so solid, the structure itself does not need to be as strong. In fact, the building materials supplied by the gospel appear almost flimsy in comparison to those at the other site. Instead of heavy framework beams, we are offered poles and rope. Instead of bricks and boards, we are given canvas. All we can do is build tents, perhaps large tabernacles.

Living within the "solid" walls of religion we will not naturally see tent dwelling as an attractive option. Instead of leaving the building, we tend to try to incorporate the materials supplied by the gospel into our religious structure, but Paul calls us out. He promises that rather than being closed in and cut off by thick timbers, we will find ourselves in airy tents that allow room to join hands with others. Sometimes we will hold hands and dance; at other times, our communities will link arms and pull together during a storm. Paul's "new-creation" tent promises the freedom to trust in and share with other people in ways that the thick walls did not allow. In Galatians, Paul invites us to put our confidence, not in religion's pillars, but in the community drawn together by the Spirit of the God who supports this canvas structure.

We often overlook Paul's invitation to leave our thick-walled religious structures. Many fail to hear Paul's invitation because of the way his letters are traditionally read. When the woman in Las Mesetas asked me if she was still saved even though she had cut her hair, I offered to study Galatians with her and the rest of the church. I perceived the problem as legalistic works-righteousness, and like many others before me, I saw Paul's letter to the Galatians as a tool to address that issue. In this book, however, we have seen that legalism is a symptom of a deeper problem, which is religion, and we have seen that encouraging works-righteousness is only one way that religion subverts holistic

Christianity and acts as a barrier to authentic community.

Certainly the common reading of Galatians can help this woman answer her specific question, but does it go deeper? Does it address the subverting power of religion? To help us answer that question, I will briefly summarize the traditional evangelical interpretation of Galatians. I base this summary not just on commentaries on Galatians, but also on notes in study Bibles, comments in one-volume Bible commentaries, sermons and Sunday-school material.[1]

The Common Evangelical Reading of Galatians

Paul's letter to the Galatians is commonly portrayed as correcting a false teaching about salvation. In his commentary on Galatians, E. F. Harrison states, "Jewish Christian agitators had circulated among these Gentile converts seeking to impose circumcision and the burden of the Mosaic law upon them as necessary for salvation."[2] Paul counters the legalism of these agitators by emphasizing God's grace. Salvation comes by faith alone, not by a combination of faith and works. When explaining why Paul wrote the letter, those who interpret Galatians in the traditional way make no mention of Paul's concern for the church as a community nor of Paul's concern for the unity of the church in Galatia. Instead they claim that Paul wrote the letter so that individual Christians in Galatia would be free from legalism and understand the correct path to salvation.[3]

Commentators commonly divide Galatians into three parts, contending that in chapters 1 and 2 Paul defends his authority, in chapters 3 and 4 he addresses doctrinal issues, and in the last two chapters he offers ethical teaching.[4]

Looking at how authors discuss a few key phrases tells much about the common interpretation of Galatians. From their perspective, the "truth of the gospel" (2:5, 14) is the principle of grace that one is not saved by obeying rules.[5] These authors discuss justification in a way that leaves the reader picturing a legal process that involves only God and the individual.[6] Merrill Tenney explains that justification pertains to our legal relationship with God. To "be justified" (2:15-17) is to be declared legally righteous.[7] Harrison states that "to be justified means to be declared and considered righteous in God's eyes, to be vindicated of any charge of sin."[8] Samuel Mikolaski adds that justification removes condemnation and guilt. A person is not justified by works of the law but by placing his or her faith in Jesus Christ.[9]

The Christian is free from legalistic rules such as circumcision. This freedom, however, must not become total license that the flesh could take advantage of. The Christian is guided by the Spirit and struggles with the "flesh" (3:3; 5:16-25) or the fallen human nature and its sinful acts.[10]

Most evangelical authors demonstrate their individualistic-spiritualized orientation by how they describe the new creation Paul mentions at the end of his letter (6:15). For them this new creation is the "spiritual re-creation of man" or when a "sinner is wholly remade."[11]

Is This an Antireligious Gospel?

The traditional interpretation of Galatians' emphasis on salvation by faith, as opposed to salvation by works, does attack legalism head-on. But it does not present the transforming power of the gospel in a sufficiently profound way. Not only does it not portray Paul as confronting the human tendency this book calls religion, it fails to appreciate the power and tenacity of religion. For example, by placing so much emphasis on a person's faith *in* Jesus Christ, it leaves the door open for religion to enter anew and focus on human action. Unfortunately, religion can seize hold of this emphasis and turn faith in Christ into a type of work that must be done in order to be saved. Performing the act of accepting Jesus Christ as Savior or believing the correct doctrines, "the truth of the gospel," can be used as religious boundary lines that can produce the same elitism and judgmentalism witnessed in relation to rules in the Las Mesetas churches.

Although the traditional interpretation's emphasis on God's grace is helpful, if the religious elements that distort people's concept of God are not addressed, the significance of God's grace is greatly reduced. It can come to mean that this angry figure is not going to hit a Christian with his big stick, at least not with the really big stick on the last day. It may still, however, leave the person living in fear of the God of the big accusing eye. An angry, distant God of grace is better news than an angry, distant God who offers no grace, but it is not good enough news. A loving God of grace is good news. The traditional interpretation of Galatians falls short of being *the* good news.

Rather than challenging the individualistic character of North American evangelicalism, the common reading of Galatians reinforces it. The argument and the language of the commentators focuses on the individual. The description they give of Galatians does not simply fall short of sufficiently confronting individualism; it in fact displays a reading of Galatians that has been heavily influenced by individualism. As the next chapter will demonstrate, this reading not only fails to see Paul's corporate concern, it also interprets individualistically a number of terms that are not primarily individualistic, such as justification and new creation.

In a similar way, this understanding of Galatians does nothing to challenge an overly spiritualized gospel. The spiritual language used, along with the emphasis placed on the individual believer's feeling of guilt and one's legal standing with God, and the way sin and new creation are discussed, all serve to reinforce a focus on individual morality and future-personal-salvation rather than a holistic gospel practiced in a corporate setting.

This understanding of Galatians does not sufficiently address the problems observed on our test drive. It does not confront religion as a barrier to authentic community. In terms of our thick-walled building analogy, we can say that the traditional reading of Galatians does help people think differently about the wall of legalism that defines the limits of the community, but it does not really cause them to think deeply enough about the idea of the wall itself. The act of having faith in Christ, or of having correct doctrine, too easily replaces the "legalistic" wall this interpretation attacks.

This reading of Galatians does not help people see how that building hinders the quality of the community they experience, nor does it invite them to leave the building and join the community under the gospel canvas. It provides limited freedom from a mistaken doctrinal approach. It does not provide freedom for community.

In reality, however, Paul's letter to the Galatians does proclaim freedom from religion and freedom for community. The following three chapters will offer a careful study of Paul's letter to the Galatians that will challenge the traditional reading summarized in this chapter. In these four chapters, talk of Las Mesetas and North American evangelicalism will recede into the background as we seek to understand Paul's letter to the Galatians. Why did he write it? What was he trying to communicate?[12] The final chapters of the book will then return to the present and discuss the implications of Galatians for us today as we explore the idea of leaving the thick-walled building of religion to experience the type of community possible only in the gospel tent.

6

The Problem in Galatia

Why Is Paul So Upset?

THE FIRST VERSES OF GALATIANS EVOKE THE QUESTION: why is Paul so upset? The beginning of this letter stands in contrast to his other letters. Instead of offering his standard thanksgiving for those he is writing to, Paul rebukes the Galatians.[1] He expresses astonishment that they have so quickly turned to a different gospel (1:6).

Paul writes to people he knows and loves. The Galatians had warmly received Paul and the gospel he preached (4:12-15). Their encounter with Jesus Christ gave birth to an active expression of the Holy Spirit, including miracles (3:1-5). Apparently, however, other teachers have arrived and their teaching distresses Paul.[2] These teachers did not seek to persuade the Galatians to abandon their faith in Jesus; they proclaimed Jesus as the means of salvation for both the Jew and Gentile. The crucial difference is that they wanted Gentile converts not only to believe in Jesus but also to adhere to Jewish laws and traditions, such as circumcision. The agitators told the Galatians that they needed to do these things in order to consummate their Christian conversion (3:3). Scot McKnight calls this a "Christ-plus-something gospel."[3] Christ was not enough; the Galatians needed Christ plus circumcision, Jesus plus certain eating habits, etc.

Why does this Christ-plus-something gospel have Paul so upset? The common answer to this question is that the Judaizers who taught this gospel told the Galatians human merit was an integral part of salvation. Paul is upset by a doctrinal error in relation to the path of salvation for individuals. He insists salvation rests on faith alone, not human works. This, however, is too narrow a definition of the problem. In the second chapter of Galatians, Paul recounts another time when he was upset by a perversion of the truth of the gospel. That incident can help us understand why he is so distressed about these teachers and their message.

Two Tables at Antioch

But when Cephas came to Antioch, I opposed him to his face, because he stood self-condemned; for until certain people came from James, he used to eat with the Gentiles. But after they came, he drew back and kept himself separate for fear of the circumcision faction. And the other Jews joined him in this hypocrisy, so that even Barnabas was led astray by their hypocrisy. But when I saw that they were not acting consistently with the truth of the gospel, I said to Cephas before them all, "If you, though a Jew, live like a Gentile and not like a Jew, how can you compel the Gentiles to live like Jews?" (Gal 2:11-14)

Paul accuses Peter and the other Jews of not acting consistently with the *truth* of the gospel (2:14). Paul gives an image that portrays the truth of the gospel—a group of people, Jews and Gentiles, eating together at one table. The contrasting image is two tables. The Jewish Christians at one table tell the Gentiles that they can join the Jews at the table if they become circumcised and fulfill other traditions. The two tables represent a tearing apart of unity in Christ. This is especially tragic since that would mean that Peter and the others not only stopped eating with the Gentile Christians, but also ceased celebrating the Lord's Supper together.[4]

Why is Paul so upset? For Paul the truth of the gospel is that "there is no longer Jew or Greek, there is no longer slave or free, there is no longer male and female; for all of you are one in Christ Jesus" (3:28). He fears that unity in Galatia is at risk. He writes to them to prevent the tragic divided table of Antioch.

This is not to say that Paul's letter to the Galatians does not address the issue of an overemphasis on human works, nor to say that what Paul writes does not have implications for individual salvation. Within the tragedy of the two tables at Antioch, there are significant observations we can make about both of these issues. (The final section of this chapter will include further reflection on Antioch.) The point here, however, is simply to emphasize that the incident at Antioch demonstrates that, for Paul, the truth of the gospel has social implications and that he has these implications, especially corporate unity, very much in mind as he writes to the Galatians. To miss this point and to read Galatians as if Paul's main concern was to show individuals how they could find a gracious God is to miss much of the richness Galatians has to offer and to misinterpret what Paul means by justification.

I have intentionally begun this study of Galatians by discussing the divided community at Antioch in order to avoid an overly individualistic interpretation of the letter. The tendency to read the letter individualistically is so strong that even many of those who acknowledge the tragedy of the segregated tables in Antioch still interpret the book as a whole, and specifically what Paul is upset about, in an individualistic fashion. Even worse are those who do not mention the corporate dimension of the problem when discussing the incident at Antioch.

J. Gresham Machen offers a significant example of this latter type of interpretation. It is significant both because of how influential he was in fundamentalism/evangelicalism and because of how he ignored and denied any hint of a corporate dimension to the problem at Antioch. Machen states that Peter's conduct led Gentile Christians into the "deadly error" of thinking there was some "meritorious work which [a person] needed to perform in order to win the favor of God." Machen makes no mention of the division of the church at Antioch having in any way motivated Paul to confront Peter. Machen's reading is so oriented to the issue of an individual's understanding of grace and works that he actually states that the separation itself was of no concern to Paul.

> If Peter had never begun to hold table-companionship with those Gentile Christians, it is not at all certain that Paul would ever have blamed him. . . . But when Peter had once accustomed the Gentile Christians to hold table-companionship with him, then his withdrawal from such table-companionship would tend to lead them to seek a continuance of their table-companionship with him by keeping the ceremonial law.[5]

Reading Galatians through an individualistic lens causes Machen to interpret the Antioch incident in individualistic terms. For Machen, the only thing at stake at Antioch was how individuals understood the way of salvation.

Sadly, even though some evangelical commentators do mention the issue of unity when discussing the tragedy of the two tables at Antioch, they tend to read the rest of the book just as individualistically as Machen did.[6] Walter Hansen is a refreshing exception. He not only observes the social dimensions of the Antioch incident[7] but includes these corporate issues in his discussion of the crisis in Galatia. The difference in his interpretation is obvious from the first page. He starts his commentary by discussing how ethnic rivalries had endangered the unity of a church he attended in Singapore. His treatment of Galatians differs, not simply because he mentions ethnic rivalries as part of the crisis in Galatia, but because he sees the issue of "the equality and unity of all believers in Christ . . . [as the] central focus of the entire letter."[8] This does not mean that Hansen places less emphasis on traditional questions, such as, is justification by law or by faith alone. Rather it means that he looks at them through a different lens and hence interprets them differently. He looks through a social/corporate lens rather than through Luther's lens of the troubled individual seeking a gracious God.

Hansen's different approach is obvious in his introduction of the section on Galatians 2:15-21:

> This social crisis in the church at Antioch was exactly the same as the crisis faced by the churches in Galatia: Gentiles were being forced to live like Jews in order to be acceptable to Jews. Behind this social crisis, however, a more fundamental theological issue was at stake: Is the truth of the gospel or is the law the basis for determining fellowship between Jewish and Gentile Christians? . . . As we work through [Paul's] theological arguments, we must not forget that he was responding to a social crisis: division in the

church along racial lines. His complex theological definitions are aimed toward the practical goal of healing this
racial division in the church.[9]

Why was Paul so upset? We can begin to answer that question
by saying that he feared a repeat in Galatia of the tragedy of the
two tables he had seen in Antioch.

Self-Righteousness, a Works Orientation and E. P. Sanders's Critique

The individualistic character of the traditional answer to the
question, Why was Paul so upset? is not the only aspect of the
traditional interpretation that scholars have challenged in recent
years. E. P. Sanders has argued convincingly that Paul did not
attack a Jewish teaching that humans earn their salvation by their
own efforts. To say he did so is to hold an erroneous view of
Judaism. Sanders asserts that common Jewish teaching, rather
than understanding that salvation was based on human merit,
stated that salvation was always by God's grace. Jews of that time
understood that God gave the law in the context of the covenant.
The law did not provide a means to achieve fellowship with God.
God had already taken the initiative and done that. The law
showed Israel how to live in covenant with God and made it
possible to do so by providing a system of atonement. They did
not teach that obeying the law was a means to earn salvation;
obedience kept one within the covenant. The issue in regard to
the law was not getting in, but staying in.[10]

If Judaism did not teach that salvation was earned through
merit-accumulating works, then the traditional interpretation is
incorrect to say that in Galatians Paul attacks a teaching which
explicitly stated that salvation is earned through human effort,
through works. How could Paul attack a teaching that did not exist?

But to say that Paul did not confront a *teaching* of salvation by works does not necessarily mean that Paul did not confront a lived-out works-righteousness. As we observed in the churches in Las Mesetas, what is taught does not always match what is lived. Evangelicals in Las Mesetas stated a doctrine of salvation by grace, but they lived as if they earned their salvation by their works. Their official teaching is an orthodox statement of the reformation faith, but they live out, and in subtle ways communicate, a legalistic religion of works-righteousness.

The fact that this occurs today in Las Mesetas does not prove that it occurred in Galatia in the first century. The experience, however, is common enough that Sanders is wrong to overlook the possibility that Paul in Galatians may address a legalism and works-righteousness that does not occur in Jewish writings but is nevertheless lived out by people in Galatia.[11] He too easily assumes that if Judaism included teaching that salvation is by God's grace, then people would not have a problem with self-righteousness or a works orientation. Rather than assuming that people will understand teaching in the most positive or grace-oriented way, we must remember that those listening to the teaching have a propensity toward "religion." Humans are inclined to think they must do things to earn God's acceptance and approval. The human religious drive leads people to distort a message of grace and continue to live as if they must earn the acceptance of God and the acceptance of others in their religious community.[12]

In the preceding paragraphs I have argued that, in describing the problems Paul addresses in Galatia, we must consider not just what was taught but also how it was heard and what was lived out. Here, and throughout this book, when I compare or juxtapose what was taught and lived out, I do not mean to communicate that teaching itself was not central. Paul was upset at the false teachers. His concern undoubtedly included what they were actually teaching. What I mean to communicate by this statement is that the problem is not "just teaching" in the more simplistic sense of the traditional reading or Sanders's interpretation. The problem is not *just* that the teachers explicitly stated "a person is saved by works." Nor is the possibility that people lived out a works-righteousness ruled out simply because the teachers in some way included words of God's saving grace in their teaching. The situation was more complex than either one of these positions imply.

I began this section by agreeing with Sanders and stating that the traditional approach has been wrong to portray Paul as being upset because the agitators in Galatia explicitly taught that salvation was based on human merit. I then, however, made a distinction between what is taught and what is lived, and I disagreed with Sanders's conclusion that Paul does not attack the practice of works righteousness in Galatians.[13]

The combination of the above two points leads to some very important observations about Galatians in relation to the churches in Las Mesetas and in relation to evangelicalism in general. The traditional understanding of Judaism and the Judaizers portrays them as explicitly teaching that one's salvation is gained through human effort. This understanding leads those who today preach salvation by grace to view themselves as "right" and to see Galatians as a corrective for others who do teach that salvation is by works. Sanders forces us all to take a new look not just at Judaism but at ourselves. Judaism and Christianity, rightly understood as rooted in God's grace, are antireligious, but they can be corrupted by religion. It is probable that the teaching of the agitators in Galatia included statements that salvation was only by God's grace. Yet Paul accuses them of not preaching the gospel. Sanders' work should lead evangelicals and others who preach that salvation is by grace to reevaluate how much we have in common with the false teachers in Galatia.[14]

This section adds to our understanding of what Paul saw as the problem in Galatia. He was upset at the false teachers, not because they were necessarily explicitly teaching salvation by works but because Paul perceived that their emphasis on following Jewish laws and traditions could split the community and easily lead people to come under the bondage of religion.[15] Under the influence of religion, the Galatians would easily misconstrue the importance of human works for salvation and standing within the community. To fail to see religion as an important issue that Paul confronts in Galatians is to miss much of the power of the book's message.

Religion in Galatians

The word *religion,* as I define it, is not Pauline. What I refer to with the word, however, is Pauline. I am "imposing" the word on Paul for ease of communication. I am not, however, imposing the ideas on him. The letter as a whole presents a contrast between a gospel rooted in God's initiative and grace and a religion rooted in human striving for status with God and other humans. The issue of religion is particularly clear in certain parts of the letter. For instance, Galatians 6:12-13 offers a picture of the teachers seeking to increase their status through success in the religious realm, the success of persuading others to follow their religious standards. It is also clear that the agitators are under pressure to measure up to religious standards themselves. Fear of persecution motivates their actions.[16] Another example is the number of times Paul emphasizes that the gospel he proclaims is not of human origin (1:1, 11-12, 16; 2:6-7). We can here say that Paul is contrasting the gospel to religion, a human construct.

Galatians 4:3-11 demonstrates most clearly that Paul sees

what I have called religion as a fundamental problem in Galatia:

> So with us; while we were minors, we were enslaved to the elemental spirits *[stoicheia]* of the world. But when the fullness of time had come, God sent his Son, born of a woman, born under the law, in order to redeem those who were under the law, . . . Formerly, when you did not know God, you were enslaved to beings that by nature are not gods. Now, however, that you have come to know God, or rather to be known by God, how can you turn back again to the weak and beggarly elemental spirits *[stoicheia]*? How can you want to be enslaved to them again? You are observing special days, and months, and seasons, and years. I am afraid that my work for you may have been wasted.

This passage communicates a number of key points that I will explore in greater detail. First, Paul equates Judaism and paganism. Therefore, on one hand the problem is bigger than Jewish teaching, but it does include at least the way the Jewish traditions were lived out. Second, both Judaism and paganism, and specific religious rules, are related to enslaving forces. Third, with regard to their relationship with God, Paul deemphasizes the importance of human action and emphasizes the importance of God's action.

The Gentile Christians in Galatia previously followed pagan religions (4:8). They have become Christians but now are turning toward following certain Jewish religious practices (4:10, 21; 5:2). Paul calls this turn toward following Jewish traditions a turn back—a return to a previous state (4:9). In saying this he has equated their observance of Jewish law with their previous observance of pagan traditions and rituals. Clearly paganism, Judaism and the teaching of the Judaizers are different. Yet Paul equates them. As tools of religion they enslave in the same way.

This observation is further supported by verse 3 in chapter 4, where Paul writes, "So with us; while we were minors, we were enslaved to the *stoicheia* of the world." Whether by "we" Paul means "we Jews" or "we Jews and Gentiles," the point is powerfully made that both were in a common state of slavery to the *stoicheia* of the world.[17] What, however, are *stoicheia*?

As commentators look at ways this word was used in earlier Greek writings they often mention the "ABCs." In Greek usage, the letters of the alphabet were the *stoicheia* or irreducible constituents of words. *Stoicheia* refers to elements that make up a series, and the word took on a wide variety of specific meanings, including the degrees on a sundial, the notes for the musical scale and the basic elements of the cosmos.[18] "Philo speaks of the Greeks who revere the four elements (*stoicheia*)—earth, water, air, and fire—and give them the names of divinities."[19] On this cosmic level, the word ties in with the religious practice of viewing the heavenly elements as spiritual beings that were active in the physical world. "From early times the stars and powers thought to control the universe were worshipped and given offerings."[20]

As with the English word *elements,* the context determines the meaning. In Galatians, some translate *stoicheia* as "basic principles" (NIV). That can seem an appropriate translation in 4:3, but Paul appears to personify the *stoicheia* of 4:9. This is especially true if we read "you were enslaved to beings that by nature are not gods" (4:8) as describing *stoicheia.* "Enslaved" is mentioned in all three verses (4:3, 8, 9), which makes it appear that the *stoicheia* are the enslaving entities referred to as "beings" in 4:8. "Basic principles" does not communicate the personal character of power Paul gives *stoicheia* in these verses. On the other hand, to call them "elemental spirits" (NRSV), while preferable, may give the impression, for modern readers, that the *stoicheia* either are uninvolved in our day-to-day life or perhaps only affect certain "spiritual" aspects of our life or certain individuals. Paul, however, writes of these *stoicheia* as if they were independent spiritual realities, yet they either are or are closely related to religious regulations that had a significant influence on day-to-day life. The translation "elemental forces" allows for this broader understanding of the *stoicheia*.[21]

Paul closely links these elemental forces and religious rules (4:8-10). It appears that these elemental forces embody or use the rules to enslave people and cause the division witnessed at Antioch. Elemental forces enslave people to the practice of religion. We might say that the spirit of religion, or the power of religion, takes up rules, which may be neutral or even good, and turns them into what I have described as religion.[22] For instance, the teachings of Judaism were not religion, in the sense that E. P. Sanders has emphasized their basis in God's grace, but under the influence of the *stoicheia,* Judaism becomes an enslaving force—religion (4:3).[23]

A simple turn of a phrase within this passage offers further evidence that religion is a fundamental part of the problem Paul addresses in this letter. He writes, "Now, however, that you have come to know God." But then it is as if he catches himself, thinking, *No, I don't want to say that. I do not want to offer them any grounds for giving importance to human actions in coming to know God.* Therefore he adds, "or rather to be known by God" (4:9). This self-correction emphasizes God's action, the exact opposite of what religion focuses on.

Why Have the Galatians Returned to the Enslavement of Religion?

In this same verse, Paul asks, "How can you turn back?" (4:9, see also 1:6; 3:1). Although we may consider it tragic, we can imagine a number of reasons why the Galatians returned to enslavement.

Juan Luis Segundo links the Galatians' actions to a general "tendency of human beings to place themselves 'under' the religious sphere." He argues that "the human being's deep awareness of its creaturely condition leads it to place religion above itself, to use the religious realm as an intermediary between the intangible transcendent on the one hand and the insecurity of its condition as a creature on the other."[24]

We can imagine that Paul gave the new converts in Galatia certain guidelines, perhaps similar to those he gives at the end of this letter, but he did not leave them with well-defined rules and rituals. Paul expected his converts to be "taught by God" (1 Thess 4:9) or "led by the Spirit" (Gal 5:18; Rom 8:14). The Galatians may have found this satisfactory when Paul was present, but when he left and they had "no law to distinguish right from wrong, and no rituals to deal with transgressions and provide reassurance, their security and self-confidence were somewhat shaky."[25] In contrast, the teachings of the Judaizers offered the security of the law, a clear way to order life and measure one's status and success within the religious group.[26]

The pressure to obtain security through religion increases when others around you are heavily involved in religion. People in the Roman world, and especially the eastern part, were very superstitious and saw themselves at the mercy of spirits and powers outside of human control. Religion offered people a small sense of control of their lives. People turned to various means, including magic, astrology and mystery cults, to escape their fate.[27]

The good news of Jesus Christ that Paul preached to the Galatians gave them freedom from religion but took away securities they had grown up with and placed them in naked contrast to others who still enjoyed the security of religion. Of course, Paul would call it enslavement, not enjoyment. The point here, however, is simply to imagine the possibility that, due to the religious environment they lived in, the structure and boundaries of the "other gospel" would have held certain appeal to the Galatians.[28]

Religion and Table Fellowship

I began this chapter by using the separate tables at Antioch to demonstrate that Paul was upset by the potential threat to unity in Galatia. The preceding sections have shown that Paul saw religion as a fundamental problem in the churches in Galatia. Now we turn to investigate the relation between religion and the threat to the unity of their community.

> Exchanges of food inevitably link persons together in webs of mutuality and reciprocity. Eating symbolizes relationships and attitudes: we eat to celebrate birthdays and holidays, we gather and serve meals to mourning family and friends at a funeral. Eating mediates social status and power: so during the 1988 presidential election, in an attempt to link himself with the "common man," blue-blooded George Bush conspicuously snacked on pork rinds.[29]

This observation by Rodney Clapp about our culture was even more true in Paul's world. The trust and acceptance communicated by sharing a meal with someone was a cultural trait throughout the Near East. Joel B. Green states that "we must come to terms with how radically sharing a meal in our contemporary Western culture differs in significance from eating together in ancient Judaism. For them, though often not for us, table fellowship was the closest form of intimacy."[30]

The incident at Antioch is not the only conflict in the New Testament over who is welcomed to the table (see, for example,

Lk 15). In fact table fellowship played a central role in Jesus' life and teaching.[31] In that era, the Pharisees had brought even more than normal attention to the table. They sought to eat every meal to the degree of purity observed by officiating priests in the temple.[32] Every Jew did not follow all the rules for purity that the Pharisees prescribed. There was, however, some spillover effect even if just in a heightened awareness of the issues. In the Pharisees' campaign to return holiness to Israel they used table fellowship as "the major vehicle of social and religious ostracism. ... To share a meal with a person was an expression of acceptance; to refuse to share a meal symbolized disapproval and rejection. Accordingly, Pharisees would not share a meal with the non-observant."[33] Although the Jewish tradition had focused on one's own purity and inclusion with the covenant people, table fellowship as an expression of religion served as a boundary line that carried an implicit rejection of those outside. For those inside, the religious boundary line around the table provided status and security.

Just as the level of acceptance and intimacy communicated by table fellowship made it a powerful instrument of religion, it also provided an effective way to challenge religion. Jesus crashed through the barriers of religion by eating with, and hence accepting, Jews whom the Pharisees considered sinners. Peter and Paul at Antioch were in a radically different situation. They ate with Gentiles. By coming together at table fellowship, by accepting Gentiles without requiring them to submit to Jewish traditions and regulations, the Christians in Antioch had made the Pharisaic distinctions irrelevant. They broke down a much bigger wall.[34]

At Antioch, Paul reacted because he saw Peter building the wall again. Peter previously sat down and ate with Gentiles. Why did he now change? It goes back to the themes Paul had emphasized. Peter did not change because of a revelation from God. He changed for human reasons, such as fear, because human messengers warned him about the circumcision faction. And those in the circumcision faction were also motivated by fear. They feared losing what had separated them from the Gentiles and thus identified them as the people of God. "The Judaizers saw their entire religion and society at threat in Paul's supposed 'law-free' gospel because he was allowing people to find God's grace without becoming socially conformed to the law."[35]

There have been efforts to help Peter save face.[36] Charles Cousar argues that the church in Jerusalem found itself under extreme pressure from Jews because of the actions of Jewish Christians like Peter in other places. Therefore, Peter, out of concern for Christians in Jerusalem, pulled back from the table.[37] Whether that was Peter's reason, or whether in fact he had a normal response to religious pressure and gave in to the fear *What will they think of me if I do not change?* is not necessarily significant. In whatever case, the root problem was separation by religious boundary lines based on human actions.

Religion: Impact on the Community and the Individual

Religion is the force that divided the table at Antioch. When Peter accepted the standards, the boundary lines urged on him by those who had come from James, he succumbed to religion. He drew a line between himself and the Gentile Christians. It communicated that the Gentile Christians as they were did not measure up to the standard. A relationship with Jesus Christ was not enough. Peter's action communicated that one also must *do* certain things, in essence become a Jew, in order to become acceptable. All of the Jews who left the table committed an act of corporate self-righteousness. At the community level, religion is clearly a force of division and exclusion.

The traditional reading of Galatians too easily misses this reality by focusing on the issue of individual salvation. Although Peter's action, and the teaching of the Judaizers, could easily lead Gentiles to think that salvation requires human effort, that was not the issue. The Judaizers were not trying to defend a message that taught one must obey all the law in order to be acceptable to God. They were trying to defend the boundary line that distinguished Jews, the people of God, from Gentiles. The question is not individualistic—how is one saved?—but corporate—who are the people of God, and what makes them the people of God? Paul correctly saw that the Judaizers' answer to that question was religious and hence destructive of the community.

This religious boundary line also, however, affects individuals. It pressures those on the outside to focus on human actions as a means of being accepted into the people of God—in short, a type of works-righteousness. Since they see some rejected for not following certain traditions and requirements, it too easily leads those on the inside to think their actions have gained them not only acceptance by the group, but also the acceptance of God. Status based on measuring up to religious standards carries with it the risk of losing status if one should fall. This fear leads to increased religious zeal, causes hypocrisy and inhibits honesty (2:4, 13; 6:12-13).

Therefore, to say that Paul wrote this letter to the Galatians in order to try to prevent a repeat of the tragic divided table of Antioch does not mean that Galatians does not address the issue of individual salvation. The religion that divides groups also enslaves individuals. To focus, however, on the issue of individual salvation will lead to too superficial a reading of Galatians. In the same way, to focus on Galatians as an argument over correct doctrine is to miss the full richness of the gospel.

Conclusion

The central question in Galatians is, what is the basis of the united fellowship of Jews and Gentiles—an encounter with Jesus Christ or rather compliance with religious standards?[38] Paul is so upset and writes with such emotion about this issue because he has observed the consequences of using human actions to define who belongs at the table. As Paul wrote this letter, he probably had two images in mind. One image portrays the truth of the gospel—a group of people, Jews and Gentiles, eating together at one table. The contrasting image is two tables. The Jewish Christians at one table tell the Gentiles that they can join the Jews at the table if they become circumcised and fulfill other traditions. Both tables offer unity, but the religious table's unity is based on exclusion. Their unity is based on how their actions have made them different from others. The gospel table offers inclusive unity.[39] It is a unity based on what God has done through Christ.

Chapter eight will explore how Paul, in writing Galatians, counters the Judaizers and their religious boundary lines that exclude some from the table. Already, however, from the exploration of the problem we know something about the solution. It cannot simply be a doctrine that corrects mistaken teaching. Correct doctrine itself does not defeat religion. In fact, we have seen that religion can seize doctrines of grace and absorb them into a system of bondage. This is not to say that teaching is unimportant. Paul demonstrated significant caution in the way he worded the phrase "or rather to be known by God." Some teaching facilitates religious bondage more than others. Seeing the depth of the problem does, however, demonstrate the need for a solution that goes deep.

7

Justification by Faith

What Kind of Justice & Whose Faith?

INCE LUTHER, MOST PROTESTANTS HAVE SEEN JUSTIFICATION, not by works of the law but by faith, as the central idea of Galatians. In the writings of Paul, Luther, a conscience-smitten friar, had found freedom from his burden of guilt and his endless striving to achieve peace with God. He used Paul's teaching of justification by faith as a corrective to the medieval church's teaching on penance and indulgences—what Luther saw as justification by works. Luther's experience has had a huge impact on the way we read Paul.[1] Protestants have not had the image of the divided table at Antioch in mind when they read Galatians; rather, using the lens of Luther's experience, they have commonly interpreted Paul as addressing the same issues: the individual's burden of guilt and a mistaken teaching of works-righteousness.

This is not to imply that a person struggling with guilt could not find release in this letter. Luther's experience was not wrong. Rather, it is wrong to use Luther's experience as the sole inter-

pretive key for the letter. The traditional understanding of justification by faith stands as a barrier to grasping the corporate
character and antireligious nature of the gospel in Galatians. A
recent Spanish translation of the Bible, *Dios habla hoy (God
Speaks Today)*, demonstrates the size of this barrier and how
firmly it is rooted in the Protestant mindset.[2]

Instead of translating Galatians 2:16 as "No one will be justified by the works of the law," *Dios habla hoy* translates it as "Nadie
queda libre de culpa por hacer lo que manda la ley" (no one
becomes free from guilt by doing what the law commands).

In nine places in Galatians, the *Dios habla hoy* version of the
Bible has translated the verb *dikaioun* or the noun *dikaiosynē* as
"freedom from guilt."[3] The translators so closely associate
Luther's reading of Paul and Paul himself that they place a
Lutheran type definition of justification in the mouth of Paul.
Instead of offering a literal translation, they place in the text their
interpretation of what "to be justified" means—to be free from
guilt. So although Paul does not even mention "guilt" or "guilty
conscience" in Galatians, someone reading this translation
would think it is a central aspect of the letter.

If we fail to provide a different understanding, it will be hard
to read the rest of the letter in a new way. Therefore, before
looking at the letter as a whole in chapter eight, I will present a
detailed discussion of this one phrase: justification, "not by the
works of the law but through faith" (2:16).

Dikaiosynē: Justice or Righteousness?

Greek Word	Latin Root	English Root
dikaios	just	righteous
dikaiosynē	justice	righteousness
dikaioun	to justify	to rectify, set right

Although not as significant a problem as the *Dios habla hoy* translation, even literal English translations are problematic. Only one Greek word, *dikaiosynē*, lies behind the two words *justice* and *righteousness*. Either is a "correct" translation, but they communicate different meanings. Whereas we usually think of "justice" in a broader social sense, we most commonly think of "righteousness" in relation to individual piety and morality. For instance, "Seek first the kingdom of God and his righteousness" may be interpreted differently from "Seek first the kingdom of God and his justice" (Mt 6:33). In the English New Testament, "righteous" and its cognates are almost always used to translate *dikaiosynē* and its cognates.[4] In Galatians 3:11 we read, "The one who is righteous will live by faith," instead of "the one who is just." The overwhelming use of "righteousness" instead of "justice" in English translations of Galatians facilitates an individualistic reading of the letter.[5] I will continue to use "justice" or "justice/righteousness" interchangeably with "righteousness" to remind us of the broader meaning of the word.

Justification, a word we commonly use, rarely appears in the Bible. Paul's statements concerning "justification" generally use forms of the verb *dikaioun* (to justify, rectify, set right).

Justification

Traditionally justification[6] is seen "as the believer's personal experience of forgiveness and deliverance from a subjective sense of guilt."[7] In contrast this section will argue that, in the words of N. T. Wright, "justification is not an individualist's charter, but God's declaration that we belong to the covenant community."[8]

A common image of justification is an individual standing before a judge and the judge pronouncing that person not guilty. Moving into the theological realm, the word *justification* leads many Christians to imagine God adjusting an individual's legal record in heaven, moving that person's name into the not-guilty column. The essence of this view of justification is captured well by the simple definition commonly taught in Sunday schools: to be justified means that, because of Christ, God can look at me *just as if* I had never sinned.

Our legal system and understanding of justice have shaped this individualistic "legal fiction" concept of justification. Our symbol of justice is a blindfolded judge using a scale to measure someone's guilt or innocence. An impersonal code of laws provides the means for the impartial judge to weigh the case. In criminal cases, others are always involved or hurt by a crime, but the central issue is one's relationship, or standing, with the law; restitution is not the focus. The aim is not to satisfy the hurt person, but to satisfy this abstract entity, justice, that hovers above us all. As we sometimes say, "The demands of justice must be satisfied." One is considered innocent or guilty, just or unjust, depending upon how he or she measures up against the abstract ideal or code.

With this understanding of justice we quite naturally think that for God to justify an individual is to pronounce him or her not guilty, that is, to view the person as if he or she had met the standard of justice. If, however, like Paul, we think about justice and justification from a Hebrew perspective, we will end up with a distinctly different image.

The Hebrew concept of justice has a relational foundation. The basis of judgment is how faithful one is to agreements, obligations or covenants with other people and with God. To act justly is to be faithful to the people one is committed to by agreement or covenant. The relationship, not an impersonal law, is central. The law, of course, is quite central for Israel in the Old Testament, but this code, in contrast to law as an abstract standard, is relational in the sense that God gave the law not as a standard to use in rewarding or punishing individuals but as an "expression of God's intention for relationships within his redeemed community." And as John Driver observes, the law was relational in the sense that "it supposed a covenant relationship in which were provisions for forgiveness and repentance and where God was gracious."[9]

Tamar provides an excellent example of the relational character of justice (Gen 38:1-26). She led Judah into fathering her sons by acting like a prostitute—an inappropriate action according to an abstract standard of right and wrong. Yet she is pronounced more just/righteous than Judah. He falls short of the Hebrew ideal of justice because he had defaulted on his obligation to her. In a related way, Israel considered God to be just/righteous, not because God met some perfect standard, but because of God's resolute faithfulness to Israel—people he had made a covenant with.

The contrast between the Hebrew relational sense of justice and our abstract concept of justice is striking at times. In Psalm 143, David admits that he is not just/righteous, but he appeals to God's justice/righteousness, asking God to not punish him and help him in his trouble (Psalm 143:2-3, 11). If today I stood before a judge, admitted my guilt and then appealed to the judge's sense of justice, you would conclude I was not thinking straight. It would be the equivalent of asking the judge to give me the harshest punishment the law allows. I would not plead for justice; I would appeal to the judge's sense of mercy. But according to the Hebrew concept of justice, David's request for God to act justly makes perfect sense. David asks God to be just, faithful to God's pact of love with David, even though David has not acted faithfully/justly.[10]

Therefore, in Galatians, when we encounter the various words with the *dikai* root we should think of justice "primarily in terms of the covenant relationship to God and membership within the covenant community."[11] Wright, in fact, suggests that "*dikaiosyne* is best translated as 'covenant membership' or 'covenant status.'"[12]

In Galatians, to be justified is not simply to be declared not guilty of having broken laws or to be placed in proper relationship with standards recorded in an impersonal code. To be justified is to be placed in proper relationship to God, to be made a full participant in the community of God's people. The individualistic image of a heavenly ledger book is incorrect. As Richard Hays states:

> There is no question here of a legal fiction whereby God juggles his heavenly account books and pretends not to notice human sin. The legal language points rather to the formal inclusion of those who were once "not my people" in a concrete historical community of the "sons of the living God" (Rom 9:25-26). (Justification is only one of the metaphors that Paul can use to describe this act of inclusion by grace; elsewhere he can speak, for example, of "adoption," as in Gal. 4:5 and Rom. 8:15.)[13]

To claim this meaning of justification in Galatians is based not just on Paul's Hebrew background but also the context in which Paul discusses justification in the letter itself—the divided community in Antioch. As Krister Stendahl states, "Paul's thoughts about justification were triggered by the issues of divisions and identities in a pluralistic and torn world, not primarily by inner tensions of individual souls and consciences."[14] N. T. Wright, with particular reference to Galatians, concurs: "The debate about table-fellowship recorded in Galatians 2 is therefore not a peripheral issue, loosely related to the real question. It raises precisely the question of justification—who is within the covenant family."[15]

The Hebrew concept of justice and the way Paul's justification language relates to the Antioch incident indicate that Paul has a corporate and social concept of justification that centers on relationship and covenant status or inclusion in the people of God. "The framework which Paul uses to locate the doctrine is social and historical rather than psychological and individualistic."[16]

To place the doctrine in this framework changes the way we think about individual salvation. As Markus Barth observes: "Justification in Christ is thus not an individual miracle happening to this person or that person, which each may seek or possess for himself. Rather justification by grace is a joining together of this person and that person. . . . No one is joined to Christ except together with a neighbor."[17] Placing the doctrine in this framework also affects the way we read Galatians. To have a psychological and individualistic concept of justification presents a huge barrier to appreciating Paul's corporate and social concerns.

The *Dios habla hoy* translation demonstrates what many people are thinking as they read the words "to be justified" in Galatians. Its translation of Galatians 5:4 clearly demonstrates the problem:

"Ustedes, los que buscan quedar libres de culpa cumpliendo la ley, se han apartado de Cristo" (you who seek to be free from guilt by obeying the law have separated yourselves from Christ). This translation and this concept of justification give the appearance that the central concern of the Galatians is to be free from guilt. If we instead insert a paraphrase of the concept of justification described in this section, the conclusion is much different: "You who seek to be included in the people of God by obeying the law have separated yourselves from Christ."

Works of the Law

Paul states that a person is not justified by works of the law

(2:16). The traditional individualistic reading of Galatians that gives little importance to the social implications of the Antioch incident and thinks of justification in terms of an abstract standard of right and wrong understands Paul to say that no one can obtain salvation by obeying the Jewish laws. The "judge" will always pronounce a guilty verdict because humans will always fall short of the standard.

The social implications of the Antioch incident and a relational understanding of justification, however, lead to a different understanding of this phrase. Paul is not thinking about justification by works of the law in an abstract sense. Rather, he is saying that a seat at the table, inclusion within the community of God, is not based on works of the law.

"Works of the law" apparently refers primarily to practices (such as circumcision, dietary laws and sabbath observance) that Jewish people used to separate and distinguish themselves from Gentiles.[18] Paul is telling those in Antioch and Galatia "that identification with the Jewish people through observances of these distinctively Jewish practices is not the basis of membership in the covenant people of God."[19]

Because these works of the law serve as religious boundary lines, or badges, there is potential for legalism, enslavement to religion and a misunderstanding of God's grace.[20] Paul's attack on religion, and here specifically on "works of the law," has implications for individual salvation. That is not, however, the primary issue in this verse. Paul attacks these boundary lines because their purpose is to separate; they have literally divided one table of fellowship and communion into two. As Markus Barth observes, "justification by works is . . . anti-social behavior."[21]

"Faith in" or "Faith of"?

If inclusion within the people of God is not based on observing

Jewish practices, what is it based on? This section will address that issue by discussing the question of how to translate "dia pisteos Iēsou Christou" (2:16). Although many translate this as "through faith in Jesus Christ" (objective genitive), others opt for "through the faith of Jesus Christ" or "through Christ's faithfulness" (subjective genitive). In the first, Christ is the passive object of human faith. In the second, Christ is the acting subject. The question becomes, does our faith justify us, or does Christ's faithfulness justify us? (This same translation decision affects other texts in Galatians— 2:20; 3:22, 26—and other Pauline texts, such as Rom 3:22, 26; Phil 3:9.) Most modern translations use the objective genitive. But over the last twenty-five years an increasing number of scholars have argued for the subjective genitive,[22] which is the way the King James Version has translated it. The impact of their work is seen in the New Revised Standard Version, which in the footnotes offers "faith of" as a possible translation.

Each side offers strong arguments for its translation, yet neither side has succeeded in convincing all (or even almost all) that its translation is the best one.[23] Since the grammatical evidence is not conclusive, in the end it is perhaps more a hermeneutical argument than a grammatical one.[24]

If one comes to Galatians with the assumption that its central message is that we find acceptance with God not by performing outward acts of obedience but by believing in Jesus Christ, then one would tend to see individual faith emphasized in the book, and hence the "obvious" translation is "faith in." I have argued, however, that that is not Paul's central message. Galatians does not focus on what humans must do to sit at the table, whether it be human works or human believing, but on what God has done to bring Jews and Gentiles together at one table (3:28). The "faith in" translation does, however, focus on the human action. It presents a contrast between two human actions by stating that a person is justified not by "A" (doing works of the law) but by "B" (believing in Jesus Christ). That is not Paul's message. As Karl Barth wrote,

> "Justification by faith" cannot mean that instead of his customary evil works and in place of all kinds of supposed good works man chooses and accomplishes the work of faith, in this way pardoning and therefore justifying himself.[25]

Those who favor the objective genitive translation would most likely state that Barth does not fairly represent their point of view. In a sense they are correct. As Hays writes, both positions "stress the death and resurrection of Jesus as the decisive act of God upon which justification depends, and both agree in regarding trust/faith as the appropriate response to this divine act."[26] Yet Barth's words, even if an overstatement, are helpful because they point to the clear difference in emphasis in the two translations. One emphasizes God's action; the other gives more room for the importance of human action. In another sense, Barth does not overstate the problem with the "faith in" translation. Even if the translators would explain justification by faith differently than Barth's description, their translation can easily be read to mean what Barth describes. Given the religious propensity of humans, a translation that encourages people to view faith itself as a work that achieves something is an unwise translation.[27]

The "faith in" translation is not only unwise in a pastoral sense today, it also appears unlikely that it reflects what Paul wanted to communicate to the Galatians. Paul, as seen by his self-correction in 4:9, understood the religious mindset. People assume they need to do something to earn good standing with God. Paul would reject the "faith in" translation because it carves out a space for human action, subtly taking a step back toward the slavery of religion. On the other hand the "faith of/faithfulness of" translation makes this verse read as the antireligious statement Paul intended it to be. It says that a person is not justified by human actions, but by God's action in Jesus Christ.

I want to be very clear that those who stress the subjective genitive (faith of) are not attempting to do away with the concept of belief or faith in Christ. Galatians 2:16 also speaks unambiguously of faith *in* Christ, an act of believing/trusting directed toward Christ as object. But this position places less emphasis on "the question of how we should dispose ourselves towards God than on the question of how God has acted in Christ to effect our deliverance."[28] This does not, however, rule out the importance of the human response to God's action.

Conclusion

Knowing that a person is not justified on the basis of works of the law but through Jesus Christ's faithfulness, we also placed our faith in Christ Jesus in order that we might be justified on the basis of Christ's faithfulness and not on the basis of works of the law. (Gal 2:16; translation by Richard B. Hays)[29]

What then did Paul communicate to Peter in this verse?[30] In essence, Paul reminded Peter that their membership in the covenant community of God was not based upon certain things they did—circumcision, diet laws, keeping the sabbath. Their status as faithful members of the community was instead based on Jesus Christ's faithful obedience to God—to the point of death on the cross. They had placed their trust in the fact that their inclusion in the people of God was based on God's action in Jesus Christ, not on obeying certain laws.

Paul did not present this as a new idea. Instead he presented it as something that they agreed on, something foundational.

His point here was that Peter's actions contradicted this truth. "The breaking up of the community created by God . . . [was] a denial of justification itself."[31]

Is "justification by faith" the central message of Galatians? If justification is understood in terms of our legal system and its impersonal laws, then the answer is no. If justification is understood in an Old Testament-Hebrew sense, then the answer is a qualified yes. More appropriately we should say that it is *one* of the ways Paul communicates his central message in Galatians.

This chapter has argued that "justification by faith" refers to the fact that inclusion in the community of God is based not on religious rules that divide but on God's initiative that brings people together. This understanding of justification by faith relates well to Paul's primary concern in Galatians—to prevent division caused by religion. Other images, however, communicate similar ideas and are just as central to the letter. For example, adoption also communicates inclusion based upon God's initiative (4:5). Freedom from the slavery of religion means the Galatian Christians do not need badges of distinction. Perhaps the most powerful images are "new creation" and freedom from "the present evil age" (1:4; 6:15). A relationship with Jesus Christ makes things new. Jew and Greek, slave and free, male and female can come together at one table.

It is therefore most appropriate to say that justification forms part of the constellation of related images listed in the previous paragraph. I wrote a whole chapter about justification by faith not because it is necessarily the most important concept in Galatians. Rather, the purpose was to redefine justification by faith so that its traditional meaning would not hinder our understanding of other concepts and images in Galatians. The next two chapters will describe how Paul uses these concepts and images to communicate the truth of the gospel to the Galatians.

8

New Creation

Freedom from Religion &
Freedom for Community

THE JUDAIZING TEACHERS IN GALATIANS PREACHED A perverted form of the gospel that threatened to divide the Galatian church and return the Galatian Christians to the slavery of religion. How does Paul respond to this situation? The problem is not simply confusion over a point of doctrine, thus the response must be more than a discussion of doctrine. Returning to the images I presented in chapter five, we might say that Paul must lead the people out of their thick-walled religious building and into the airy gospel tent. For this reason, I suggested that freedom from "the present evil age" and "new creation" are key images in Galatians (1:4; 6:15). The cross breaks into this age and makes things new. Paul wanted the Galatians to live in the reality of this new creation.

Freedom from religion is only part of what Paul calls freedom from the present evil age. As Jacques Ellul writes, freedom from the present evil age is freedom from every lordship except that of Jesus Christ. Ellul lists a number of examples, including freedom in relation to the state, to mammon and to sociological pressures of conformity.[1] Therefore, in discussing Galatians in terms of the theme of freedom from religion and freedom for community, I do not mean to imply that this covers all that Paul communicates in Galatians. It does, however, have a prominent place in the letter, and I will focus on the issue of religion since that is a theme of this book.

Paul wrote this letter to an actual group of people who were going to listen to it read in one sitting. It is "a situational proclamation focused on the anticipated aural event in which God will cause the gospel to invade the edition of the present evil age that is current in Galatia."[2] J. Louis Martyn rightly places significant weight on the importance of this aural event. He invites us to attempt "to take [a] seat in a meeting of a Galatian congregation," to imagine how they would hear this letter and then to move back and enter into Paul's active anticipation of the theological event the letter will cause. "Paul wrote Galatians in the confidence that God intended to cause a certain event to occur in the Galatian congregations when Paul's messenger read the letter aloud to them."[3] Paul wanted the Galatians to experience the gospel of Jesus Christ anew in such a way that the Judaizing message would lose its appeal and become obviously unnecessary. The alternative was slavery to religion and its divisive boundary lines.

Galatians 1:1-5: God's Initiative Provides Freedom from the Counterfeit Community of the Present Evil Age[4]

Paul an apostle—sent neither by human commission nor from human authorities, but through Jesus Christ and God the Father, who raised him from the dead—and all the

members of God's family who are with me, To the churches
of Galatia: Grace to you and peace from God our Father and
the Lord Jesus Christ, who gave himself for our sins to set
us free from the present evil age, according to the will of
our God and Father. (Gal 1:1-4)

Paul wastes little time in getting to the issue at hand (1:6).
That does not mean, however, that he simply scribbles off a
standard greeting to fulfill the custom of that time. His saluta-
tion is brief, but through it, especially in the few phrases
unique to Galatians, he begins proclaiming freedom from
religion and freedom for community. The very first sentence
of his letter makes a point he will stress repeatedly—the gospel
he preaches is not of human origin.[5] This emphasizes a central
theme in Galatians—the gospel is rooted in God's action.[6] The
gospel is something totally new. In contrast, religion is a
synthesis of human values borrowed from the society, human
religiosity and human constructions of how a God or gods
would operate.

Hellenistic letters commonly began with the word *greetings*.
Paul instead starts with the phrase, "Grace to you and peace from
God our Father and the Lord Jesus Christ." Paul may have meant
that as a prayer for the readers or as a blessing—a performative
utterance that actually conveys God's grace to them. Either way
it highlights a central truth of the letter: God has graciously taken
the initiative to bring peace and reconciliation.[7]

Only in Galatians, however, does Paul expand this prayer/
blessing with a compact narrative summary of the gospel he
proclaimed. J. Louis Martyn's vivid translation captures the
apocalyptic sense of this rescue operation: " 'Who gave up his
very life for our sins,' so that he might snatch us out of the present
evil age" (1:4).[8] In Jewish apocalyptic traditions, the history of

the world is divided into "two ages": the present age of corruption and the age to come, when God's justice will finally be established. Paul proclaims to the Galatians that, as a result of Christ's death on the cross, they have been liberated from the destructive power of the world as they have known it.[9]

Thus right from the start of the letter, in the greeting itself, Paul points to Jesus' death providing not just forgiveness of sins but a profound and complete freedom—including freedom from religion and the counterfeit community it produces. Paul sets the stage not to discuss the fine points of appropriate religious boundary markers but to contrast religion with something totally distinct—a community produced by the gospel of Jesus Christ.

Galatians 1:6—2:14: Religion Produces Division and Judgmental Communities

Paul immediately makes it clear to those listening that he considers the teaching of the agitators a perversion of the gospel (1:6-9). The first two chapters communicate that Paul knows this perversion, religion, very well and has seen what it produces. Paul reminds the Galatian listeners of his "earlier life in Judaism" (1:13-17). He had invested great energy in a religious distortion of Judaism. His zealousness for the traditions of his ancestors led to a violent attempt to destroy the church of God. In contrast to his human striving to maintain religious boundary lines, Paul states that God acted "through his grace . . . to reveal his Son" to Paul so that he might cross those religious boundary lines and proclaim the gospel to Gentiles (1:15-16).

In describing the episode of the false believers in Jerusalem, Paul equates the truth of the gospel with freedom, and he equates the religious motivations of the judgmental "spies" with slavery (2:4-5). As we have already noted, Paul also accuses Peter of not acting according to the truth of the gospel when he stopped eating with the Gentile Christians in Antioch. Peter's fear of the circumcision faction caused him to draw a religious boundary line that ruptured the church's fellowship.

Paul has implicitly linked the Galatian Judaizers' "Christ-plus-something gospel," which added conditions one must comply with to be a "true Christian," with his religiously motivated persecution of Christians, with the spies in Jerusalem and with Peter's actions in Antioch. What did their religious boundary lines lead to? Persecution, communities of fear and shame, destruction of the church of God, enslavement and division.

Galatians 2:9-10: Authentic Community Reaches Across Former Lines of Separation

Paul also communicates to his listeners that the pillars of the church had accepted the very message the teachers in Galatia are disputing (2:9). If the church leaders did not compel Titus, a Gentile, to be circumcised, would they treat the Galatians differently? The leaders in Jerusalem asked only one thing of Gentile Christians (2:10). Upon hearing those words the Galatians must have been sitting on the edge of their seats thinking, *Maybe the teachers are not totally wrong.* What was the one rule or tradition they would have to follow?

The one thing was that they help the poor (2:10). That is not an item religious boundaries are often built on. In fact, in this case it even crossed boundaries. The leaders were probably referring to the money Paul collected for the poor in Jerusalem. The Jewish Christians asked Gentile converts not to follow Jewish traditions, but to demonstrate solidarity with others in the Christian community—Jewish Christians! Religion had led to persecution and judgmental attitudes toward those outside the boundary lines. The liberating action of the cross of Jesus Christ led to reaching across boundary lines to help the needy. Since the

Galatians had participated in the offering for Jerusalem, Paul is reminding them that they already are part of this Christian community. The church leaders have already accepted them, and the Galatians have acted upon that.[10]

Galatians 2:15-21: Alienation Produces Communities of People Who Hide Behind Religious Masks

Unfortunately the agreement in Jerusalem did not stop the questioning about what Gentile Christians needed to do to be full-fledged members of the Christian community. Peter's actions in Antioch and the teaching of the agitators in Galatia demonstrate that it persisted. Paul's strong words against Peter communicate to the Galatians how seriously Paul takes this matter. Just as he reacted vigorously against Peter, in this letter he reacts vigorously against the Galatian perversion of the gospel. He tells Peter and the Galatians that justification is not by works of the law but by the faithfulness of Jesus Christ (2:16). They are included in the people of God because of the action of God.

We must place Paul's words about sin (2:17-18) in the context of the Hebrew sense of justice/righteousness. A "sinner" is best understood not as one whose acts cause him or her to fall short of a standard of perfection but as one who does not trust God and thus is in a state of alienation—estranged from God, self and others. The acts we call sins are fruit of these distorted relationships.

Like Adam and Eve we refuse to trust God and believe that what we are—finite and vulnerable human beings—is good. We refuse to believe that God and others love us as we are. In our estranged state we often experience feelings of fear, anger, shame or loneliness. We carry a sense of insecurity in the depth of our beings. Like Adam and Eve, we grasp fig leaves to hide our finiteness from others.

For some, this cover-up takes the form of striving to be more than just human, to stick out above others. Some respond to the insecurity or shame they feel because of their finitude by pulling back or hiding. Whether we express our distorted relationship with others by seeking to stick out or by pulling back, or by a combination of both, our alienation from God and others hinders us from living at peace with ourselves.[11]

Religion offers a sense of security in response to this lack of peace. It gives humans definitions of what is good and provides measurable ways to excel and gain approval. Religion, however, gives a static solution that does not provide deep peace or invite one to become the unique person he or she is, in relationship with others. Religion provides fig leaves, or masks, ways to cover up our finiteness. Masks stand in the way of authentic community.

By providing masks as the solution to the human sinful state of alienation, religion only exacerbates the problem. Justification, on the other hand, does not offer a cover-up, but goes to the root and provides restored relationships with God, oneself and others. The faithfulness of Jesus Christ not only provides the means of justification but also models and enables (2:20) appropriate human relationships. In Jesus, God in human flesh, we see a human being who totally trusted the Father and therefore could accept and embrace his humanity rather than reject finitude by grasping or hiding.

Paul states, "But if I build up again the very things that I once tore down, then I demonstrate that I am a transgressor" (2:18). If Paul returned to using rules and rituals as religious dividing lines he would demonstrate himself a sinner, a transgressor on a number of levels. He would be trusting in religious acts of distinction rather than in God's love (2:20) and justification through Jesus Christ (2:16), and hence he would live in alienation from God. Rather than accepting his human finiteness, he would be seeking to hide it behind a mask of religious superiority that defines others as inferior. For Paul, to transgress is not so much to break a rule but to fail to live according to the new reality produced by the cross of Christ.[12]

Galatians 3:1: Community of the Cross or Community of Religious Glory?

Paul now turns to address the issues in Galatia directly. As in 1:6, his strong words surely caught the listeners' attention: "You foolish Galatians! Who has bewitched you? It was before your eyes that Jesus Christ was publicly exhibited as crucified!" (3:1). We might ask, why does Paul here and throughout Galatians center on the cross rather than the resurrection?[13] Not, of course, because he did not believe in the resurrection; rather because he knew the danger of what Luther called a theology of glory. Although I have said some critical things about Luther's reading of Paul, I applaud Luther for following Paul in keeping the cross central and rejecting a theology of glory.[14]

By *theology of glory* Luther meant a theology that focuses on and speculates about the unseen awesome majesty of God's glory. Its source is not revelation but the human mind; theology of glory describes how people imagine a god ought to be. Many conceive of an all-powerful god one must bargain with through sacrifices and good works. A philosopher or theologian may use terms such as immutable, omniscient, omnipotent and impassible to describe God, and a Sunday-school teacher might sing, "Be careful little hands what you do." A theology of glory is a theology of the impersonal, distant "Supreme Being."

In contrast to a theology of glory a theology of the cross springs not from the human mind but from God's self-revelation in Jesus. The gracious action of God expressed through God's taking on human flesh and suffering with and for humanity clashes with human notions of how God ought to be. Luther stresses the contrast between the two approaches when he exhorts:

> You must not climb up to God but begin where he began—in his mother's womb he became man—and deny yourself the spirit of speculation. . . . You should know no God at all apart from this man, and depend upon his humanity. . . . In this matter, of how one should treat God and act towards God, forget about speculation about his majesty. . . . We know of no God excepting only the incarnate and human God. . . . If you are concerned about your salvation, forget about all ideas of law, all philosophical doctrines, and hasten to the crib and to his mother's bosom and see him, an infant, a growing child, a dying man. Then you will escape all fear and errors. This vision will keep you on the right way. . . . To seek God outside Jesus is the Devil.[15]

To seek God outside of Jesus is a grave error because, as we saw in chapter two, when people perceive God as distant, angry and accusing, then a religious lifestyle of seeking to appease this threatening power is a natural response.

A theology of glory is also a serious error because many people attempt to diminish their sense of insignificance and vulnerability, their finiteness, by linking themselves with a glorious and powerful God. That link provides people with an illusion of grandeur, but in reality, it is a rejection of their true selves and thus increases their state of alienation and their enslavement to religion. One must perform religious rites and obey religious rules so that God will reward with glory rather than punish with anger.

In sum, a theology of glory is a religious theology of alienation. It leaves one alienated from oneself and from a distant God of glory. A person feels at peace with this God only when he or she performs adequately. The relationship is not rooted in love. A theology of glory, linked arm in arm with religion, facilitates the formation of a community of fear, conditional acceptance, shame and relational superficiality. It, therefore, alienates people from the other members of their community.

Paul proclaims a gospel of Jesus Christ crucified, a radical contrast to a theology of glory. Paul's theology of the cross presents a suffering God who took the initiative to restore the breach with humanity. Thus it subverts religion instead of facilitating it. God, as revealed in Jesus, does not provide the supposed security of a theology of glory, but God's justifying action in Jesus Christ replaces it with relationship, a relationship with the God revealed in Jesus and with others in the people of God.

Galatians 3:2—5:1: Community Formed by God's Initiative

In the verses that follow (3:3-5), Paul attacks a common religious reversal of the gospel. The gospel places the initiative with God. Religion tells people they must act first—that God's action is conditional upon human action. Paul reminds the Galatians that they did not receive the Spirit through works of the law, but through the proclamation of the gospel.[16] The presence of the Spirit was a clear sign of their inclusion within the people of God. This inclusion was not, nor presently is, dependent on human works of the law.

This one powerful argument is enough to prove Paul's point (3:2). Paul could stop here. The fact that he continues communicates again to us how seriously he takes this issue. He wants to remove any doubt. However, it also displays that Paul does not just want to win an argument. He recognizes the strong grip religion has on people and the large barrier religion is to a community of love. Through the letter itself, he desires that they once again experience the freedom from the "present evil age" that a restored relationship with God provides. He is not just trying to win a debate about what is necessary for conversion; he wants the Galatians to live differently—according to the truth of the gospel.

In the rest of chapters 3 and 4 Paul develops a number of themes that reinforce and elaborate ideas he has already communicated. He emphasizes that Gentiles are included, and were meant to be included, in the people of God (3:8, 26-29). He uses Abraham to make this point, the very figure his opponents probably used to stress the necessity of circumcision. Paul also points out that the covenant with Abraham predates the law. It is rooted in God's promise, not in the law (3:17-18; 4:21-31).

Just as Paul begins and ends this letter stating that the work of Jesus Christ has created a new reality, throughout these two chapters he repeatedly depicts Christ as the central actor (3:13-16, 22, 26-29; 4:4-5, 19; 5:1). The centrality of Christ's work is especially significant if we continue to translate *pisteos Iēsou Christou* in a way that emphasizes Christ's faithfulness rather than human faith. For instance, Hays translates the end of 3:22 as "so that what was promised might be given through the faithfulness of Jesus Christ to those who believe."[17]

Paul proclaims the results of Jesus Christ's faithfulness in dying on the cross, but he does not explain *how* Jesus' death and resurrection bring about new creation and justification. He does not offer a theory of the atonement, and for the purposes of this book, we can follow Paul and proclaim rather than explain.[18] In order, however, to fully understand Paul and Galatians we must avoid the common error of limiting our understanding of what was accomplished on the cross to one explanation, such as understanding the cross only in terms of a legal transaction by which Jesus pays the penalty for our sin. This explanation tends to produce an individualistic understanding of the atonement. We do better to keep in mind the variety of images that Paul uses to refer to Christ's saving work on the cross. For instance, in Galatians we see the apocalyptic sense of the cross as a victory over the powers, producing a new creation (1:4; 4:8-10; 6:14-15).[19] Yet, in images like "adoption" (4:4-7), Paul makes it clear that the significance of Christ's work was not just at the cosmic level. It provides salvation for individuals who are adopted into God's family. The faithfulness of Jesus has implications at the cosmic, corporate and personal levels.

Galatians 3:28: Community Without Barriers of Separation
Whether Gentile or Jew, the "children" are adopted into the same family. The Judaizers' questions about what Gentile Christians must do to enter the Christian community become insignificant in front of the claim, "There is no longer Jew or Greek, there is no longer slave or free, there is no longer male and female; for all of you are one in Christ Jesus" (3:28). Although all can agree with Luther that "these are magnificent and very glorious words,"[20] a community-oriented reading of Galatians, rather than the traditional individualistic one, will see them as not only glorious but central to Paul's argument.

First, this verse points to the cosmic consequences of God's action in Jesus Christ.[21] Jesus' death ushers in a new age that transforms the very structure of reality. Christians, being in Christ and having been clothed with Christ (3:27), enter into this new age.

Second, this verse highlights the difference between religion and the Christian faith in regard to the individual and the group or community. Religion requires community for defining and enforcing rules, but the action required to enter and remain in the community is individual compliance with rites and rules. The religious community is made up of people who meet the standards. In contrast, the gospel Paul preached produces a community that brings individuals in, not because of what the individual has done, but because of Christ's faithfulness, which has led to the destruction of the barriers of separation.

Therefore, if we think that Paul is upset with the teachers at Galatia because they have misconstrued the path an individual must take to receive salvation or experience freedom from guilt, we have not, in fact, understood the letter. If we use Galatians to argue that an individual must have faith in Christ, not works, to be justified—to be included in the covenant— we may be on the same road as the teachers at Galatia. A focus on religion necessarily leads to a central concern with an individual's actions. A focus on the individual may just as necessarily lead to religion.

Paul's emphasis on Christ's faithfulness means that to believe is to recognize that one is "in." Belief is not the step that earns entrance; the Christian is in because of what Christ has done. Belief is trusting that Christ has erased the boundaries. To believe in Christ is to live in that truth. If Paul had said, "It is not circumcision but faith in Christ that marks entry into the covenant," he would have been offering a new religious system, a new way to set up barriers of separation. Instead, Paul argues that Christ has destroyed religion and its boundary lines.

Some may think I have overstated this attack on religious barriers and boundary lines. One could ask, "Don't all communities have some sort of boundary markers that separate them from nonmembers?" Yes, both a religious community and a "new-creation" community will have boundary markers that help define who is part of the community, but the character of these boundaries is decidedly different. Returning to our building image, we observe a thick wall that surrounds the religious building and serves as a boundary of separation. In contrast, no barrier surrounds the "new-creation" tent—the tent itself does not even have sides. Even so, one can still differentiate between those inside the tent and those outside. Both communities have means of defining who is "in," but the means are so different they have very little in common.

One passes through the gate of the religious wall by measuring up to certain standards. The religious community members know they must continue to meet the standard in order to stay within the wall. All depends upon their actions. The wall communicates a spirit of exclusion; the breezy "boundary" of the tent communicates a spirit of invitation. One can enter not because she has successfully met a standard but because Christ has provided the means of entry. It is noteworthy that the activities or rites that most clearly differentiated Christians from non-Christians— baptism and the Lord's Supper—signify something God has done.

A Christian, in response to God's action of inclusion and adoption, will act decidedly differently from those outside the tent. It is not, however, the actions that keep the Christian inside the tent; it is the relationship with the Spirit of Christ and other Christians. Actions of a certain character flow from that relationship and help identify someone as a new-creation tent dweller. Actions of a different character are produced when someone is out of relationship with God and other Christians. Although these actions may identify that person as having crossed a boundary and being outside the tent, an action did not cause the boundary crossing; a broken or distorted relationship with God caused the movement out of the tent. Religious or sinful actions flow from an estranged relationship with God and thus demonstrate that one is outside the tent. If someone's actions show that person to be outside the tent, the communities' response is not so much just to demand correct behavior but to help the person return to proper relationship with God and others.

We can imagine that at Antioch Paul considered Peter outside the tent—acting in a way not consistent with the truth of the gospel. Paul addresses the behavior itself, but his words to Peter are rooted in a discussion of relationship—justification by Jesus Christ's faithfulness. In this same incident at Antioch, we can see that one of the distinctive aspects of the new-creation community, that is, one of its boundary markers, is to not use boundary lines of a religious character. When Peter separated himself from the Gentile Christians, he communicated through his actions that they had to meet certain requirements in order to form part of the family of God; he had begun to build a wall. Hence he was not living as one in the new-creation tent.

Freedom from religion is a characteristic that serves as a boundary marker of authentic Christian community. It is much harder to define how a person stands in relation to that boundary, however, than to determine on which side of a religious boundary line a person stands. In part, this is because what we would have to measure is attitudes not just actions. Recalling our tithing example from chapter two, we know that two people can do the same thing for very different reasons. One person with a religious attitude will give to achieve, to measure up; another person will give out of gratitude for what he or she has received.

Although, as we will see in chapter 6 of Galatians, Paul defines some actions as Christian or non-Christian, tithing, and many other actions, cannot automatically be categorized as a religious boundary line or as a new-creation boundary marker (see 5:6; 6:15). To reiterate, both communities have boundaries, but one way of defining the boundaries comes from the present evil age and the other from the new creation. The character of the boundaries is so different, it may be better not even to use the same words to describe them.[22] As the letter proceeds, Paul continues to contrast communities rooted in these two ages.

Galatians 4:1—5:6: Freedom from Religion and Adoption into a Radically Different Community

We have already seen how in Galatians 4:1-11 Paul identifies not just pagan religion but also Judaism as enslaving religious forces. In contrast to the slavery of religion, Paul offers freedom through Christ (5:1). Instead of slavery and division, Paul offers the image of family, children of God, who, in friendship, do not judge and divide but accept (4:5-7, 12-15, 31). One is adopted into this family because of what Christ has done, not because one observes special religious regulations (3:26, 29; 4:5).

In using the image of adoption, Paul is reinforcing what I have called the most powerful images in Galatians: "new creation" and freedom from "the present evil age" (1:4; 6:15). For Paul, adoption is not a sentimental image of rescuing a needy orphan. It is an image of the transforming impact of God's action in Jesus Christ. As Rodney Clapp states:

> When children are adopted they take on new parents, new siblings, new names, new inheritances—in short, a new culture. And those who have been baptized into Christ, according to Paul, have been adopted by God. This baptism means that Christians' new parent is God the Father. Their new siblings are other Christians. The new name or most functional identity is simply "Christians"—those who know Jesus as Lord and determiner of existence. The new inheritance is freedom and the bountiful resources of community. Their new culture, or comprehensive way of life, is the church.[23]

In this new culture there is no longer Jew or Greek, slave or free, male or female. These religious, social and economic divisions are gone (3:28); circumcision is unimportant (5:6; 6:15). But the teachers' and the Galatians' use of circumcision and religious celebrations to separate who is in and out makes them extremely important for Paul—so much so that he can make the shocking statement, "If you let yourselves be circumcised, Christ will be of no benefit to you" (5:2).

It is very hard to understand this extreme statement if you view Galatians as a discussion about works-righteousness. One can imagine listeners thinking, *Wait a minute, Paul, maybe we have put a little too much emphasis on these Jewish traditions, but we do have faith in Christ; it's not that bad.* If, however, one reads Galatians in the way we have set out to, then Paul's statement is quite appropriate. By accepting circumcision as a religious boundary line, the Galatians return to the present evil age. They live as if the cross had not happened. They submit to something Christ has shown to be beggarly and weak (4:9). Sadly, they rebuild walls Christ has torn down (3:28). If, in Christ, Gentiles are heirs to the promise, religious rules of inclusion become irrelevant. It is like telling people already inside a stadium watching a football game that they have to buy a ticket to get in. They already are in!

Galatians 5:7-12: Religious Community and the Offense of the Cross

Jesus was crucified, in part, because he offended the religious leaders of his day by not living up to their expectations of glory and by tearing down their community's religious walls of separation. Paul recognized that the cross continues to offend. It clashes with a theology of glory and contradicts the basic premises of religion. To preach circumcision is to remove the offense of the cross (5:11).

Paul understands that his message is offensive and upsetting to those anchored in this present evil age, but it amazes him that someone who has tasted freedom in Christ would return to the old way (3:1; 4:9; 5:7). Although Paul still awaits the complete expression of the gospel he preaches (5:5), he does not view the gospel as simply a ticket into a future paradise where all things will be new. He says in the present tense that in Christ there is no longer Greek or Jew because he has experienced the new age by gathering at a table to eat with Jew and Gentile, male and female, rich and poor, slave and free. He knew the yoke of slavery to religion; he has experienced freedom from it in Christ. The gospel produces a new community where religious lines have been erased.

9

New Creation

*An Ethic of Freedom for
Christian Community*

IN GALATIANS 1:1—5:12 PAUL HAS UNDERCUT AND DEVASTATED
the "other gospel" of the agitators. Those listening were surely
impressed, but Paul's unrelenting emphasis on God's action
and his uncompromising attack on religious works may
actually have left some wondering if his opponents were right.
The Judaizers had probably told the people that Paul's teaching
was good, but that it was not enough. He needed more
emphasis on rules to prevent inappropiate behavior. These
teachers, besides linking obedience of Jewish laws and
traditions with inclusion in the people of God, probably also
taught that the law is necessary to control behavior. They
feared that without the law people would indulge the flesh.[1]

Galatians 5:13-16: Loose-Living Community?
Paul directly addresses their accusation in the verses that follow:

For you were called to freedom, brothers and sisters; only do not use your freedom as an opportunity for self-indulgence, but through love become slaves to one another. For the whole law is summed up in a single commandment, "You shall love your neighbor as yourself." If, however, you bite and devour one another, take care that you are not consumed by one another. Live by the Spirit, I say, and do not gratify the desires of the flesh. (Gal 5:13-16)

Freedom is a central theme for Paul, but it is freedom from slavery to powers of the present evil age, like religion. Freedom is not an autonomous independence that means a person can do as he or she wants. Our individualistic society and modern Enlightenment framework has often led me to confuse independence and freedom. At times, I have taken what I called a step of freedom, but actually it was a move of independence—avoiding a situation that would limit my ability to do what I wanted to do when I wanted to do it. For Paul, freedom does not diminish our commitment and responsibility to others, but enhances our ability to become slaves of love to each other.

Contrary to what the agitators may have said about Paul, he makes clear that he is not against the law. He gathers the law together under the command to love one's neighbor and then links this loving behavior with the Spirit. Through these statements, Paul communicates that freedom from slavery to the law does not mean a freedom with no direction or orientation. The Holy Spirit provides direction and guidance.[2]

Thus the contrast for Paul is not so much law or no law, but a law of love and the Spirit versus a religious use of the law. The latter gives the appearance of ethical superiority, but produces a community of mutual destruction (5:15). There may be much activism, strict moral behavior and good deeds, but without the freedom of Christ these actions are too often motivated by fear of what others will think if one does not perform them or by the desire to prove one's worth to God and others (1:10; 5:26). Those motivations will poison the actions they produce. "There is no love without freedom."[3]

Paul's emphasis on freedom does not imply a watered-down form of Christian behavior. It is exactly because of Paul's message of freedom that he can expect a greater level of love and unity in a Christian community than in a community enslaved to religion (5:13). As Norman Kraus says, "Paul's message is that Christ frees us from alienation and hostility, and destroys barriers of religious legalism so that we can relate to each other without these things."[4] In the rest of the letter, Paul describes how the Galatian churches might live out this freedom to love.

Galatians 5:13—6:10: Can a Community Have Nonreligious Ethics?

Paul's exhortation about life together contains a number of imperatives. Is Paul adding on to the gospel just like the Judaizers and their Christ-plus-something gospel? How can someone who has written so negatively about his opponents' use of the law hand out his own list of imperatives and write positively about the law of Christ? After combating religiosity throughout the letter, does Paul now end up contributing to it? Is Paul just switching one set of religious rules for another?[5] Absolutely not, the antireligious character of the letter continues. After tearing down the religious walls of division, Paul now shows us how to discuss ethical behavior in a way that does not lend itself to becoming a Christ-plus-something gospel.

Paul's imperatives and ethical discussion differ from the religious rules of the agitators in four significant ways. First, the context, or the way the content is presented, affects the contents.

Paul has spent more than four chapters telling the Galatians they are not justified through the law or by their own actions. The context of grace and freedom will affect the way the Galatians hear these imperatives. Whereas religion desires to tell the Galatians that fulfilling certain requirements will make them "true Christians," members of the covenant people of God, Paul's emphasis on their justification through Christ's faithfulness would make it difficult for them to hear Paul's imperatives as a condition for inclusion.

The order of the material in the letter, indicative before imperative, is not accidental. As Markus Barth observes:

> A solemn transition from proclamation to exhortation, from indicative to imperative statements, from *kerygma* to *didache,* from gospel to law, from dogmatics to ethics—this topical shift has been observed in the external structure of several Pauline Epistles and also in many individual Pauline affirmations. This sequence and procedure appear essential to Paul's teaching. Before God demands anything of man he gives grace and salvation. When new life, obedience, discipline and suffering are described, a consequence of justification by grace rather than a precondition or corollary of salvation are in mind. Works of obedience are the fruit of the Spirit, not merits establishing a claim upon God or righteousness.[6]

The imperative flows from the indicative. As we have seen throughout the letter, God's action precedes human action. Religion communicates the opposite: do something (human action) so that you can receive something from God (God's action). In their indicative context, Paul's imperatives are not religious rules.

God's action, however, is more than just a stimulus to human action. Paul says to the Galatian Christians that because of Christ's faithfulness they are part of the people of God; but he also tells them that through the Spirit they have the possibility of living as the people of God. The *fruit* of the Spirit contrasts the *works* of the flesh, not just in a moral sense but also in how they come about. Paul encourages the Galatians to live by the Spirit (5:16, 18, 22, 25). The Spirit enables them to follow Christ's example, become slaves to one another and bear each other's burdens— fulfilling the law of Christ (6:2).[7]

The second way Paul's imperatives differ from religious rules is that his concern to encourage the Galatians to live out who they are in Christ gives his imperatives a character different from religious rules, which function to create boundaries and to provide members clear ways of measuring their success. Religion needs specific rules whose compliance is easy to judge or measure (for example, you either are circumcised or you are not; you celebrate a special day or you do not; you eat with Gentile "sinners" or you do not).[8] Few of Paul's guidelines in this section are measurable in the way religion requires. Paul's lists, especially the positive one, do not lend themselves to boundary making. For instance, one can easily separate those who eat with the uncircumcised from those who do not, but dividing those who love their neighbor, avoid envy or demonstrate gentleness from those who do not is not done so clearly. Paul's ethical approach in this letter differs significantly from his previous Pharisaic pursuits.[9]

Third, rather than imposing a static list of comprehensive rules, Paul places his confidence in the Spirit. He expects the Spirit to guide the Galatians in their ethical actions (5:25).

Fourth, the image of fruit not only serves to contrast Paul's ethical guidance with what religion would offer, it also reinforces his assertion that Christians are free from the present evil age. Paul is not just talking about updating or retooling a list of rules.

The fruit comes from a completely different tree with a new root system. This is not the "roots" and "tree" of the present evil age.[10] Paul's imperatives differ from the religious rules he critiques, not just because they are worded differently, but more importantly, because they are rooted in something totally different.

Galatians 5:16—6:10: Community of the Flesh or Community of the Spirit

It is not just that Paul discusses ethics in a nonreligious way. He, in fact, continues to be on the attack against religion. A closer look at Paul's use of the terms *flesh* and *Spirit* will allow us to see more clearly how the antireligious nature of Paul's argument carries over into this section as well.

The contrast between flesh and Spirit parallels Paul's contrast between the present evil age and the new creation. His use of flesh and Spirit also demonstrates continuity with his contrast between what is merely human and God's activity in other parts of the letter. Barclay explains that "Paul is not concerned here with a 'fleshly' part of each individual (his physical being or his 'lower nature') but with the influence of an 'era' and its human traditions and assumptions. . . . The Spirit is not less than the divine power unleashed in the dawning of the new age, the source of new life (5:25)."[11] In the terminology of this book, we could say that one of the things at issue here is what determines life in this community: the "fleshy" human religiosity, common to the present evil age, or an antireligious framework provided by the Spirit?

By highlighting *religion,* I do not mean to imply that the term summarizes in a comprehensive way all that Paul discusses in this section. The main point is that when Paul here uses the terms *flesh* and *Spirit,* he points to something much broader than just a struggle between two "natures" within an individual human.

This broader conflict does, however, include a transformation that provides freedom from the enslavement to religion, which then has significant consequences for the life of the community. The linkage between "flesh" and religion is explicit earlier in the letter. Paul asks the Galatians, "Having started with the Spirit, are you now ending with the flesh?" (3:3).[12] Religion does not account for all the vices Paul associates with the flesh. It can, however, be associated with more than half the list, including idolatry, sorcery, enmities, strife, jealousy, anger, quarrels, dissensions, factions and envy (5:19-21). Religion is part of the present evil age, part of the desires of the flesh, that enslaves individuals and threatens the unity of the community. In contrast, freedom from the present age allows a community of the Spirit characterized by love, joy, peace, patience, kindness, generosity, faithfulness, gentleness and self-control (5:22-23).

Throughout the epistle, Paul has emphasized the participation of Christians in and with Christ as a way to defuse the argument of the teachers and to provide the basis for all coming together at one table (2:19; 3:14, 16, 27-29; 4:6-7; 5:24). Paul is longing for Christ to be formed in them (4:19). What would it mean to have Christ formed in their midst? What would it mean for the Galatian community to be formed in the image of Christ? Paul has answered those questions in 5:13—6:10, perhaps most specifically by encouraging them to bear each other's burdens, to follow Christ's example and to become slaves to one another, working for the good of all (5:13; 6:2, 10).

Although it may be appropriate to differentiate this section of the letter as the ethical portion, in reality, ethical and theological concerns are intertwined throughout the letter. Paul's disagreement with Peter was not simply a disagreement over doctrine, nor is Paul's theological statement of oneness in Christ devoid of ethical implications. More important than defining what is ethical and what is theological is to recognize that Paul's concern for community and the theme of new creation pervade the entire letter. This new creation is not automatic. Chapters 5 and 6 demonstrate that Paul recognizes that the present evil age continues as a reality that lures and tempts believers.

In conclusion we can say that to pronounce imperatives, to talk of the law of Christ and of slavery to one another, does not conflict with the freedom Paul has proclaimed earlier in the letter. Rather these actions are an expression of that freedom. The freedom of the gospel is a freedom from the present evil age and hence a freedom from the slavery of religion. Also, however, as freedom from the present evil age, it is freedom to live differently from what is natural, what is of the flesh. It is freedom for authentic community, freedom to bear one another's burdens in a community where there is no longer Jew and Greek, slave and free, male and female.

Galatians 6:11-18: Conclusion

Galatians contrasts human action rooted in this present evil age with God's action in Jesus Christ, which produces a new creation. The conclusion of the letter, written in Paul's own hand, highlights these main themes.[13]

In these verses Paul describes the agitators as operating from a religious framework (6:12-13). It is a picture of people using religious rules as a means to cover up the insecurities they feel because of their state of alienation. They are not at peace. They are worried about what others think of them[14] and fear persecution. In contrast to what Paul has described in the previous verses, they have not responded to the Gentile Christians out of love. In seeking to avoid the offensiveness of the cross, they are a threat to the community.

The agitators seek the glory of religious success. In contrast to these human efforts, Paul roots himself in a totally different framework (6:14). He does not boast of human effort but of God's action—an action not of glory but of the cross. In that crucifixion is new life. In contrast to mistrust and estrangement there are restored relationships; in contrast to slavery there is freedom from religion. This means the drive to cover his human finiteness with masks has died. Paul is free to love.

Almost the final words of the letter are "neither circumcision nor uncircumcision is anything; but a new creation is everything" (6:15). In essence he is saying to them, "If you have not yet understood, let me make this very plain: this is not about one set of rules or another. The issue is whether you are rooted in the present evil age or in the new reality created by the cross." How strange this must have sounded to those so committed to the "fleshy" religion of the present age. We can imagine them thinking to themselves, *Wait a minute. I thought he was against Gentile Christians' getting circumcised. Did he just say it does not matter?* From a religious point of view, what Paul said does not make sense; rules that supply boundary lines do matter. In his letter to the Galatians, however, Paul has proclaimed freedom from the enslaving power of religion and its divisive boundary lines. He has told the Galatians that this freedom, grounded in God's action in Jesus Christ, provides the possibility of living together as a community in a totally new way.

10

Responding to Religion Today

THE EXAMPLE OF LAS MESETAS REVEALS HOW RELIGION subverts holistic Christianity and acts as a barrier to authentic community. Although religion, as symbolized by a thick-walled building, offers a sense of security and binds people together into a community, the pillars, beams and internal walls—constructed out of things like legalism, individualism and spiritualized teaching—make communication, connection and caring difficult. The outside walls of exclusion—based on rules and correct beliefs—cause people inside to feel fear and shame and produce graceless communities of conditional acceptance. Together, the internal and external walls foster a community of relational and ethical superficiality.

These observations lead to the question: How do we leave the thick-walled religious building and experience the community of the "new-creation tent," where we can trust and share with other people in ways that the thick walls do not allow?

The exposition of Galatians offered in the previous chapters is an excellent place to start. Those in a Christian community, however, will receive the full benefit of Paul's teaching only by accepting the possibility that Paul would arrive at our churches and say, "I am astonished that you have turned to another gospel." We must read it as a message for us. Are we so different from the people Paul wrote to? They had experienced salvation by grace and were, even the agitators, still preaching that salvation was by grace through Jesus Christ. Instead of immediately placing ourselves with Paul on the "right" side of this debate, we will profit more if we ask how we are like the Galatians and the agitators and let his words challenge us as they challenged the Christian communities in Galatia.

We can make many connections between Galatians and our churches today, but the religious version of Christianity found in North American evangelicalism has very significant differences from the churches in Galatia. Our churches are not dividing over circumcision. Individualism and "the Great Reversal" were not part of the "present evil age" when Paul wrote. Therefore we must not just repeat Paul's message but also learn from his model and approach as we address our situation today.

Removing Obstacles and Opening Doors

A group of ten North Americans recently spent a week with us in Honduras. They came to further a relationship their church had established with a church here in Tegucigalpa. During our last meeting together, a number of people from the group shared how their lives had been profoundly touched or altered significantly. That in itself is not surprising; experiencing a reality so different from the United States affects most visitors. What impressed my wife and me so much, however, was the depth of feeling these people expressed and that many of the things they mentioned were not things we would have predicted or listed as "objectives" of the trip. Although we could say they had occurred because of the program we set up, we had not programmed them. For instance, we had included times when a person from each church would tell his or her life story. We saw it as a way for the churches to get to know each other. Two people, however, shared that telling their stories had brought significant healing to their lives. Others spoke of gaining a new understanding of themselves or Christian community through an evening with a Honduran family, sharing communion or a work day together. I listened in awed surprise at the potential of very simple things—relationships, observation, interaction, personal sharing—and of the power of God's Spirit to work through those things. It was beautiful to observe, but I knew I could not capture it or program it to happen again. The Spirit blew, and will blow, where the Spirit pleases.

A religious community can be programmed; a new-creation community is a thing of relationships, of process and, most of all, of the Spirit. We cannot offer people a package of information, "eight steps to new-creation community." Like Paul, however, we can seek to remove obstacles to the Spirit—pointing to something and saying, "this is not new creation but is of the present evil age." And we can seek to open doors to the Spirit's blowing.

Determining what obstacles to attack and what doors to open is best done through prayer, reflection and conversation in a given setting. The following is a list of some possibilities.

Just as Paul stated "this is not the gospel," we can help ourselves and others by differentiating religion from the gospel. Then we can address specific aspects of the religious version of Christianity common in our churches. For instance, to expose the Great Reversal removes an obstacle; to present a more holistic model of ministry opens a door to the Spirit.

Individualism is deeply embedded in our society and churches. If people do not even become aware that they are wearing individualistic lenses, there is little chance of their changing their ways. Simple things, like looking at individualistic misreadings of biblical texts, can begin to remove this obstacle. Just as Paul took care in how he said things (Gal 4:9), we can lessen our individualistic language and open a door to the Spirit's guiding people in a more corporate way. For instance, we can evaluate our models of evangelism and our overuse, perhaps, of the phrase "personal Savior." How can we invite people not just to a personal relationship with God but to participation in a community of the Spirit? Dislodging common images of justification and new creation, and replacing them with the less individualistic images described in this book, is a simple but significant way to remove an obstacle and open a door.

An important door to open is, like Paul, to proclaim freedom from the present evil age and to offer the possibility of something quite different. Perhaps like Oscar from Amor Fe y Vida Church we can say, "Wouldn't you like to be part of a church where . . ."

Human action, earning God's approval by our deeds, is at the heart of religion. It is a natural tendency, and we must constantly counter it by making clear how the gospel of God's initiative through Jesus Christ is different and then, like Paul, talking about ethics in a nonreligious way. Human action lies not just at the heart of religion but at the heart of evangelicalism. Our rage for goodness, for doing the right thing, merits further reflection.

Getting to the Heart of the Matter

Although evangelicals would readily agree with Paul that God's action, not human action, is the basis of Christianity, most of us operate differently. Paul spent the first two-thirds of his letter talking about what God has done and only then turned to talk about human action and behavior. In contrast, many of our sermons, Bible studies and Sunday-school curriculums spend much more time talking about what we ought to be doing than about what God has done. And often when we do talk about God, it is in the spirit of making sure we have the right information and believe the right thing—this, in reality, is still human-centered religion. Central to our ethos is to be right in word and action. Evangelicals have a rage for goodness that makes morality central to our version of Christianity.

Which would be more upsetting in many evangelical churches—if it came to light that an elder was in a relationship of adultery or if it came to light that one of the elders lived as if acceptance by God and others in the church depended on one's church attendance, tithing and moral behavior? Paul was apparently more upset when he wrote this letter to the Galatians than when he wrote a letter to a group of Christians in Corinth who had significant problems in the area of moral behavior. That should cause us to pause and reflect.

Understandably, we will do whatever we can to prevent people we love from hurting themselves through inappropriate behavior. Unfortunately, however, many evangelical parents, Sunday-school teachers, youth group leaders and pastors use God in a threatening way to lend more weight to their moral admonishments. Even if we might not like to admit it, as a way of ensuring right behavior many of us implicitly or explicitly communicate an image of God as an accusing figure ready to punish a misdeed. We do this even at the risk of contributing to someone's having a mistaken concept of God.

We must pay attention to what we observed in those Las Mesetas churches that have been the fruit of our mission efforts. The legalistic Christ-plus-something gospel so evident in these churches calls us to evaluate how prevalent a Christ-plus-something gospel may be in our own churches. Like the churches in Las Mesetas we state a gospel of grace, but what do we live out? Do we also communicate conditional acceptance? Are people in our communities also afraid to speak honestly of their struggles and failures?

The search for security through being right and acting right is not a recent addition to evangelicalism, but today there is a new sense of urgency not only to guard the morality of the church but to take up the cause of guarding the nation's morality. As Dwight Ozard states:

> These days . . . American evangelicals see themselves, primarily, as guardians of values and virtues. Christianity, if you listen closely to the leading voices of the new evangelical establishment, is a means to an end, one part of a journey toward (re)creating a better America. Ironically, these conservative evangelicals have become what theological liberals were earlier this century, equating faithfulness with morality (private or public) and replacing the gospel's mission of outreach and regeneration with a public righteousness and (often divisive, name-calling) civil religion. . . . Better politics and values may make us more popular and America a *nicer* place to live, but they won't rescue American evangelicalism, or restore it to faithfulness.[1]

Improving the nation's, or one's own, behavior is a good cause, but it is not Christianity. You may find it difficult to agree with my statement, but think about it this way. Is God more interested in having a loving relationship with us or in having us behave well? You may prefer not to answer the question or to say "both." But it is important that we give an answer. How would an earthly parent answer it? Is it more important to me that my daughter obeys all the rules or that we have a relationship of love? Clearly

I do not want her to engage in practices that hurt her, but it would be horrible to have a daughter who kept all the rules but did not talk to me.

I ask these questions, however, not because God is making an either/or choice but to bring to light how our rage to be right clashes with Christianity. Our willingness to sing "Oh Be Careful Little Hands," a song that can communicate that God is an accusing figure ready to punish children who are naughty, demonstrates that we have, even if unconsciously, placed the priority on behavior rather than relationship. I am not simply saying that we need more "balance." If we consider relationship central as God does, it will change the way we talk about Christian behavior and ethics. It is at this point that we must read Paul very carefully and take very seriously that Galatians is much more than a tract about salvation by grace rather than works.

Even though our religious practices may be good things, just as the Judaizers in Galatia viewed their practices as good things, when they come from the framework of religion they are rooted in the present evil age. The point here is not the action itself. For instance, one can attend church motivated by religious reasons. In that context, church attendance is seen as part of a system of rules that is imposed on you. A person attends for fear of how God and others will respond if he or she does not or with the hope of receiving something from God if he or she does. There is nothing Christian about that attendance; one could behave with the same motivations in a social club or political party. In contrast, one can attend in the freedom of the new reality brought about by the cross. The desire to attend comes from within and is rooted not in rules but in relationship with God's Spirit and others in the Christian community. Paul calls us to live in the latter framework, to be rooted in the Spirit rather than the flesh.

Paul states the gospel in such a radical way that people would ask, "Does that mean we do not have to do anything?" Perhaps we are not preaching the same gospel Paul did if no one asks us that question. Paul's answer to the question is no (Gal 5:13), but he is very aware that this is the exact point where religion will seek to regain lost ground.

Having the yoke of slavery to religion lifted off one's shoulders brings both a sense of relief and freedom but also nervousness and insecurity. Paul recognizes a person's tendency to want to return to the familiar security of religious boundary lines. Therefore, as we saw in the previous chapter, when Paul writes about ethics and behavior, he does it in a decidedly nonreligious way. We can say that his ethics gives people building materials that do not lend themselves to use in a religious building.

We must follow Paul, not just in the way that he avoided giving rules whose compliance could be easily measured, but also in having our imperatives grow out of the indicative. As Robert Hill said, "Paul . . . was ever answering the question of what we should do by saying something first about what God has done."[2]

Having grown up singing "Be careful, little hands, what you do" and judging my neighbors by whether they mowed their lawns on Sunday, it does not come easily for me to change the way I preach, teach and talk about Christian behavior—even as convinced as I am of the problem of religion and a focus on human action. Among the things I have done is to set the goal of always including an indicative element and a word of grace anytime I address an ethical issue. Also, when I find a preacher who gives indicative sermons that talk about ethical issues in a way different from what I am used to hearing—that is, they talk about our actions as response to God's action and use words like *possibility* more than *ought*—I seek to read and listen to them as much as I can.[3] I also seek out theologians, like Jacques Ellul, Vernard Eller and Christos Yannaras, who intentionally discuss ethics in an antireligious fashion.[4] These sermons and books help me be self-critical about my religious tendencies and give me the language to talk differently about Christian behavior.

Yet I continue to be amazed at the tenacity of my religiosity. Perhaps the saddest and most ironic is when I find myself feeling superior because I am not in bondage to religion like others. As soon as I say that in a self-righteous way, I *am* in fact in the grasp of religion. We must continually recognize our religious tendencies and hence deflate them by naming them. It is much more dangerous to think we have come totally clean of religion, when, in fact, it always lurks within us. As David Gill once suggested to me, we should go to church with a certain sense of humor. We should smile at ourselves as we see the religion we practice.[5] That exposes religion for what it is, a now-defeated power, and it leaves us depending on God's grace. Then, with Paul, we can make statements like the following:

> May I never boast of anything except the cross of our Lord Jesus Christ, by which the world has been crucified to me, and I to the world. For neither circumcision nor uncircumcision is anything; but a new creation is everything! (Gal 6:14-15)

But Our Actions Are Important!

If you are anything like me, one of your responses to the last section is probably "Sure, I see the point. Human-centered religion is not the gospel, but haven't you gone a little too far? Our actions, what we do, are important; the Bible places a lot of emphasis on a changed life."

I have placed significant emphasis on including more of an indicative character in our teaching and preaching, but my point is not just that we need to talk more about grace and less about doing. We need to talk about ethics in a totally different context—that of new creation instead of the religion of the present evil age. The aim is to deemphasize a religious approach to ethics, not to deemphasize ethics.

Granted, through pressure and an imposed system of rules, religion produces significant superficial changes. Admittedly, an antireligious emphasis may lead to less compliance on this level, but is that necessarily bad? Think, for instance, of personal devotions. Through religious pressure, there were times in my life when I read my Bible and prayed for a few minutes every day because I felt I *should*. It was a combination of measuring up to the standard of what it meant to be a good Christian and the influence of the almost superstitious/magical attitude that you might have a bad day if you did not do your devotions.[6] Inevitably, however, I would miss a day or two, feel guilty and then return to the practice, trying to exert more willpower and feeling even more pressure. Would you want to have a relationship with someone who visited you for a few minutes a day because someone else obligated him to visit you? Since I have felt freedom from the religious pressure to do my devotions, there have been times that my Bible reading and prayer life has been inconsistent, and at other times it has been as consistent as before. Qualitatively, however, it is different. Even if at times I return to a very structured schedule of devotions, it does not feel like I am simply checking off a box on my list of Christian obligations. Rather, I commit myself to a more regular devotional life because I see it as a positive aspect of my relationship with God—I want to do it. I have been freed from doing devotions out of a sense of obligation or an attitude of religious bargaining and freed to have a more sincere and meaningful relationship with God.

So in relation to certain actions like church attendance or having devotions, a religious approach may produce greater compliance. But an ethic of freedom facilitates a qualitatively superior action. When we move past superficial behavior, religion hinders profound change, as we saw in relation to rules about marriage in Las Mesetas. A new-creation community both expects and facilitates more significant change.

God as Revealed Through Jesus

A person's religiosity and his or her concept of God are intertwined. Equally important as attacking religion is correcting the distorted concept of God that facilitates or causes a religious approach. Instead of implicitly accepting or promoting the distant God of the big accusing eye as a helpful tool in keeping people in line, we should invite people to form their concept of God by looking at God's self-revelation in Jesus. Was Jesus quick to condemn and accuse? Did he carry a "big stick"? Did he create shame or heal shame? Significantly, Jesus' harshest words were reserved for those who themselves were accusers who drew religious boundary lines.

Someone may offer the challenge, "What about the Old Testament God of wrath?" But there are not two Gods, just one God. If one looks at the big picture in the Old Testament, not just focusing in on moments of judgment, he or she will find the same God of love that is found in the New—a God who is slow to anger, long on patience and mercy, and amazingly faithful; a God whose anger is an expression of love, not in competition with love.

Experiencing that love as an individual defuses religion's power and offers the foundation for authentic Christian community. I intentionally use the word *individual*. Paul's concept of community, a body, is more than just a collection of independent individuals. And as the next chapter will explore in greater detail, a key element of authentic Christian community is that each member of the community experiences God's love.

11

Individuals & New-Creation Community

THIS BOOK HAS INCLUDED A SIGNIFICANT CRITIQUE OF individualism. In North America the religious version of Christianity has absorbed the extreme individualism of the society, and thus individualism has contributed to the subversion of biblical Christianity and become part of the religious barrier to authentic Christian community. Individualism is part of our present evil age.

Also, however, a number of times during the book I have added phrases such as "this does not mean that individual salvation is unimportant." Those phrases may have appeared as simply an attempt to protect myself—a line I had to put in to keep some readers from putting the book down. That is not the case. The Gospels are full of examples of Jesus' bringing salvation and healing to individual persons. Nothing Paul writes leads me to think he had less concern for individual people. My commitment to Christian community does not conflict with my commitment to express God's loving acceptance to individuals. Rather, authentic Christian community requires people whose lives are not an expression of alienation and distorted relationships with God and others but persons who have experienced God's reconciling love. I know this from experience. The following is just one example of it in my life.

Alienation Blocks Community

To enter the world of doctoral studies at a major university is, like in many jobs and professions, to enter into a situation where one feels constant pressure to improve one's status among the scholars of the field. Those who have already achieved their degrees seek status by giving papers at conferences and publishing books and articles. Other scholars measure them not only by how much they have published, but by which publishers and journals publish their work. Not yet at that level, graduate students hope that impressing a renowned professor with a great paper will help them move off the bottom rungs as they begin to climb the academic ladder to success, but mostly, on a day-to-day basis, they feel the pressure to impress others by comments they make in seminars.

In my first days in graduate school I was not so much reaching for a higher rung on the ladder as trying to figure out how to demonstrate to others that I was even on the ladder. For a variety of reasons I perceived myself as being at the bottom of the group of first-year students. I longed to show that I could speak intelligently about theology, but I lived in fear of saying something that would confirm what I already felt—I was not really in the same league as the other students. Usually the fear won out and I sat quietly in seminars.

One particular moment portrays well the way I felt and acted that fall. It was midsemester and I had not said anything in a particular seminar. One day the professor mentioned something that reminded me of a certain theologian. Part of me wanted to seize this opportunity and demonstrate I was "well read," but my shame-driven habit of silence seemed to push a "mute" button. I said the name in a whisper, but the professor, perhaps reading my lips, repeated the name and affirmed the connection I had made with what he was talking about.

The atmosphere over lunch in the student lounge was, of course, more relaxed. I talked with other students, but still there was a sense that I was hiding. I said some things as a way of covering up and did not say other things for fear of what they would think of me. Then one day in a different seminar, the guest speaker said something that so disturbed me I spoke out before the image-protecting part of me could hit the mute button. It was not a statement that was calculated to impress anyone; I simply reacted. Everyone remained silent after I spoke. I immediately assumed that what I had said was so dumb that people did not even know how to respond. To make matters worse, all of the theology professors attended this seminar. I wanted to crawl under the table. In a moment, someone made another comment, and the discussion went off in another direction.

After the seminar I went not to the student lounge but out into the parking lot, fleeing my shame. But I started praying. I thought about the cross and the extreme shame Jesus experienced. I continued praying with the confidence that God understood what I was feeling, and I sought to rest in God's love for me. That allowed me to be compassionate with myself but also to reflect honestly about my drivenness to impress others and hide my perceived weaknesses.

Those moments of prayer did not give me a permanent freedom from the pressures I felt; I was still reserved in most seminars, and I prayed similar prayers many times in the remaining three and a half years in graduate school. But one thing did change: I felt enough security in God's love to begin speaking honestly with other students. As I told them how I felt, I was surprised to find that they experienced the same doubts and fears. In moments of vulnerability the suffering and scared part of me connected with the suffering and scared part of others, and friendships of deep solidarity were formed.

The contrasting image is a person who, in the words of Frederick Herzog, "seeks security in external things . . . [and] has built a wall between his true self and the pseudoself he displays."[1] Wearing masks and presenting a pseudoself means one is not in open relationship with others. It is a counterfeit community of one pseudoself talking to another pseudoself.

Christian community entails much more than a couple of graduate students standing in the hall sharing their fears about approaching oral exams. But this story does demonstrate clearly the link between a person's experiencing peace with God, dropping his mask and having richer relationships and more authentic community. The connection between a person's resting in God's loving acceptance and authentic community is not limited to graduate students struggling with shame.

Over the last couple of years, I have repeatedly recalled a quote by church historian Roberta Bondi because it makes so clear the connection between a person's resting in God's love and expressing love to others.

> Peace is a deep disposition of the heart. It is humility, an ability to let go of the need to be right in our own eyes or the eyes of others, an ability based on the knowledge that our rightness or wrongness in any issue is totally irrelevant to God's love for us or for our neighbor. The peace that

comes with claiming our self in God is the foundation of
our ability to carry God's reconciling love to others in the
most humble places and humble everyday ways.²

The flip side of Bondi's words is that if people are not secure
in God's love, their alienation from God will lead them to live in
ways that hurt others. Some people are so alienated from God
and others that they respond to people around them with violence and abuse, or exploitation and manipulation. Included also
in this flip-side description are some who are very "good" and
may perform tremendous acts of charity and service to neighbors.
If these good deeds flow from a person's insecurity, as a way to
be noticed or gain approval, than the action itself will be tainted.
The helper's need to be needed will get in the way of offering the
help her neighbor needs most deeply. Paul would tell her that she
has gained nothing (1 Cor 13:3)—not in the sense that her good
actions failed to qualify her for merit points with God; the actions
have gained nothing in relation to establishing relationships of
love in an authentic community.

I have stressed that in our individualistic context we need to
recover the corporate nature of justification and understand it as
inclusion in the people of God. For our corporate life together,
however, we each need to experience justification. Through justification in Jesus Christ, we are returned to a relationship of trust
and love with God. In the security of that relationship, we have the
freedom to drop our masks and live as the vulnerable, finite humans
that we are. That, in turn, provides freedom for a community of
people to relate honestly and sincerely with each other.

Not Just Milder Individualism
Individualism is a barrier to authentic community, but expressing
concern for a person's relationship with God does not clash with

a commitment to community. That does not mean, however, that the solution to individualism is to simply talk a little more about community and a little less about individuals. A qualitative, not just quantitative, change is needed. A new-creation community is "new" not because it has a little less individualism but because it provides a new way of understanding personhood.

As I explained in chapter four, the individualism of the present evil age tells us that one's true self is what is at the core of one's being, independent from others. Individualism prizes self-sufficiency and independence. The Bible presents a different concept of true personhood. A person's true potential, or true self, is found in interdependence and the sharing of concern for others.

Evangelizing individuals or expressing pastoral care to one person does not automatically conflict with authentic community. At issue is the concept of salvation and concept of the person that one communicates. Is it a "salvation" that reinforces the individualism of the society, or is it an invitation to a new creation where the person finds his or her self-identity as a person-in-covenant community?

The present evil age offers autonomy and independence; the gospel of Jesus Christ offers freedom for covenant community. It is a freedom from alienation from God and hence a freedom from our self-alienation, freedom from the hiding we do to cover up our finite humanity and the grasping we do to try to become more than just finite humans. It is freedom from the powers of this evil age, such as materialism, racism, sexism and individualism, that alienate us from ourselves and others. The cross of Jesus Christ produces a new creation where one is freer to express loving commitment to others and thus experience his or her true personhood.

Paul's concept of justification includes much of what I have covered in the last two chapters. Although many have misinterpreted his use of the term, Paul certainly was correct to use it in the midst of a discussion of authentic Christian community. Through the faithfulness of Jesus Christ, we are justified and included in a covenant community. We are not just declared "innocent" but brought into commitments with God and others. Thus Paul's view of justification requires and expects more of us than a "legal fiction" concept of justification. Our justification through Jesus heals and restores our relationship with God and others. Therefore we can live out our commitment to the community in an atmosphere of openness and compassion rather than one of fear and judgment.

Conclusion

This book began with concrete examples of communities produced by religion. I later represented the character of religious communities by comparing them to a thick-walled building. In contrast, I presented the distinctly different image of a community living under a large tent. Rather than being closed in and cut off by thick timbers, in airy tents Christians can join hands with others, sometimes to dance, at other times to pull together during a storm. In Galatians Paul invites us to put our confidence not in religion's pillars but in the community drawn together by the Spirit of the God who supports this canvas structure. A "new-creation" tent promises the freedom to be open, honest and trusting of other people in ways that the thick walls do not allow.

The new-creation tent is a beautiful image. What, however, does an actual new-creation community look like? To answer that question, I would like to take you back to Las Mesetas to visit a church that, through reflection on Paul's letter to the Galatians, has sought to leave their thick-walled religious building and live in the reality of the freedom from this present evil age provided by the cross of Jesus Christ.

As you recall from chapter three, Amor Fe y Vida Church began because a group of Christians wanted to practice a holistic gospel and were unable to do that in the churches they had been attending. The leaders felt it was both imperative and urgent to encourage the whole congregation to embrace a holistic gospel. They asked me to give some seminars that would move people toward a commitment to a holistic gospel. We agreed, however, that a workshop on how to interpret the Bible would be the best place to start. It was in the midst of that workshop that the woman raised her hand and asked if she was still saved even though she had cut her hair. In response we studied Galatians together for a number of weeks. Our plans to have workshops on a holistic gospel were delayed.

Studying Galatians with Amor Fe y Vida Church spawned the central ideas of this book,[3] but my writing was not the only fruit of our study of Galatians. It had a significant impact on the church. The results were dramatic, but not everyone would call them positive. In fact, after studying Galatians, they looked very much like a group of people who were trying to figure out how to live together in a tent after years of living in a heavy-beamed building with its neatly partitioned rooms and halls. The immediate confusion was over rules. All agreed that the religious legalism they had lived under was not Christianity, and some were eager to throw out all the rules. But when a few of the teenage girls started wearing makeup and slightly shorter skirts, some church members began to try to figure out how to have some of the old rules without being legalistic. Others wanted to replace the old rules with a new list of "standards" that placed an emphasis on helping others in the church and the outside community. Although this original scurrying around has settled down, they are still, a few years later, trying to figure out how to live in a tent. But rather than pressing to settle the above issues "once and for all," they are coming to see that living in a new-creation tent means their security and settledness will never be spelled out in a clear-cut system like the one they left. Their security and peace will be in their relationships with God and each other.

Rather than focusing on writing down a new set of rules that will apply to all those in the church, they find their discussions about behavior and standards focus on individual situations. For instance, all the other churches in Las Mesetas simply draw a line and say that no one in a common-law relationship can be baptized, partake in the Lord's Supper, lead singing, teach or even collect the offering. Amor Fe y Vida Church wants to promote marriage, but they also have wrestled with what it means to love the women in their church who live with non-Christian men who refuse to marry them. The church decided they would not simply label the women fornicators and force them into the role of spectators at church. The church leaders evaluated each case individually. They found that many of the women in question were much better spouses than some of the people in the church who are legally married. The church now decides if someone can participate as a leader not on the basis of the legal status of his or her marriage but on how the person lives out the relationship with his or her spouse. Once Amor Fe y Vida began looking more closely at each person's situation, the church also became more active in counseling and assisting the people in their relationships with their spouses and children.

The strictness of the legalistic churches of Las Mesetas gives the appearance of producing significant changes in people's lives. They accuse those from Amor Fe y Vida of being worldly and preaching "cheap grace." Yet as we saw in chapter two, besides the negative fruit of their religious rules, such as divisions, fear, shame, self-righteousness and distortions of people's image of

God, the religious rules impede profound change. Recall the example from chapter one of the woman who was a member in good standing in her church, a Sunday-school teacher, because she fulfilled the churches rules—she was legally married. Yet she does not live with her husband and admits they have a lousy relationship. Her church offers rules, but those rules do nothing to challenge or help this woman and her husband.

At the same time that Amor Fe y Vida was "loosening" rules in individual cases of people in their church who are not legally married, the church was increasingly sobered by the sorry state of relationships between spouses in their church and community. They did not pronounce new rules. Rather they asked the couple who seemed to have the best marriage in the church to begin to lead discussions on Thursday nights on how to improve one's marriage. This was a hard and painful step. A number of the church leaders themselves had problem marriages. It would have been easier for them to simply continue feeling content with the fact that they were obeying the standard rules of being legally married and remaining faithful to their spouses. Their freedom, however, called them to go beyond the rules.

Attempting to build a Christian community without a religious foundation has led to more than simply evaluating the rules they inherited from their religious past. In their discussions about ethics and Christian behavior they find themselves talking about new issues. Unlike the other churches in Las Mesetas, Amor Fe y Vida discusses the destructive power of consumerism. And they find themselves talking about old issues, destructive forces like alcohol, drugs and sexual promiscuity, in a different way that does not simply label them as religious taboos.

A teenage member of the church was being pressured by his friends to drink beer. He asked Jorge, the pastor, if it was a sin to drink. Jorge responded that he could not really say that drinking was a sin, but he could give a number of reasons why this teenager should not drink. Jorge talked about his experience as an alcoholic and all the suffering it had brought to his family. He shared that his alcoholism had started by drinking beer with friends as a teenager. Jorge asked the teenager to think about the places where people drink in Las Mesetas, at parties or bars, and the fighting and violence that takes place in these environments. He also reflected with the teenager about reasons people drink in Las Mesetas—many drink as a way to escape problems at home or find release from emotional stress. Drinking does not bring a solution, but brings greater economic and emotional pressure. Jorge helped the teenager move past the simple question of a rule about drinking, and that teenager does not drink today.

The people of Amor Fe y Vida Church believe that the solution to alienation with God and others is not religion but trusting in God's justifying action in Jesus Christ. They have shifted from a religious approach that discouraged openness to a relational approach that provides more space for vulnerability. For instance, one father I'll call Carlos told me that he used to feel perfect when he was obeying all the rules at his former church, but it was superficial, not a true perfection. Giving the appearance of religious perfection was the goal. He told me he did things so that others would be impressed, and he never talked to others in the church about his weaknesses and struggles, only about victories! He notes a difference now in Amor Fe y Vida. Last year he and his wife had difficulty with a rebellious son. Carlos's first instinct was not to tell anyone in the church. He did not want to ruin their image of being a good Christian family. But instead of living according to his old pattern, he and his wife talked with the church leaders about their son. The leaders offered ideas that Carlos and his wife found helpful.

A young woman told me that she finds fewer inner divisions

and attitudes of superiority in Amor Fe y Vida Church. In the church she previously attended, she felt that unless she excelled in keeping the rules and working in the church she would not get to be part of the church's elite group whom she saw as the true Christians, the ones who would go to heaven. This woman has become a very active leader at Amor Fe y Vida, but she is motivated by a different Spirit.

How has this "detour" through Galatians affected Amor Fe y Vida's original goal of moving the whole church to support a holistic gospel and to help the poor in the church and the neighborhood? Like any detour it slowed them down, and unlike most detours, it has actually taken them to a place different from where they expected to go. That is to say that now, as they are actually engaging in social action, the programs have characteristics they would not have expected a few years ago. For instance, they have set up a scholarship program to help twenty children from the church and community pay the small, but prohibitive for some, cost of going to public school. They were not satisfied, however, to just give money to help the children go to school. More aware of the way sin and alienation have distorted and destroyed relationships in many families, they set up the program in a way that included elements to help the parents improve their relationship with God, with each other and with their children. As the program leaders become more involved with the families, they have encountered more challenges. Since the church does not respond to the problems with either religious condemnation alone or physical aid alone, the scholarship program has become harder to run. By many measures it was more "successful" the first year.

That comment could be made about many aspects of the church. Life in the new-creation tent has made life in their Christian community more complex, messier and less successful in terms of numbers or appearances. They have not yet arrived. Although they seek to follow Paul and place the emphasis on God's loving action and have their ethical discussion and actions come as a response to that, at times they lapse into old ways. There are many issues they are still working through, and they long to come closer to the ideals that led them to start the church. But two things are clear. They are experiencing a richer level of Christian community than they did when they went to churches firmly built on a religious foundation and preaching an individualistic-spiritualized gospel; and they have not used their "freedom . . . for self-indulgence" (Gal 5:13). When they came out of the thick-walled religious building and became more transparent and vulnerable with each other, they became more aware of each other's needs. Therefore their freedom has led to a greater involvement in each other's lives. In fact, they have demonstrated what Paul makes clear: freedom from religion is freedom for an increased level of Christian commitment; it is freedom for community.

Notes

Introduction

[1]From a letter by Robert Ekblad to the author, December 21, 1994. The pastor is from a Cristo Misionero church near Minas de Oro, Honduras.

[2]Before that time the only Protestant presence in Honduras was limited to the North Coast in areas that had been under British control. Those churches ministered primarily to English colonists and other foreigners. The exceptions to this were mission efforts among the Miskito Indians by the Anglicans in the mid-1700s and later more successfully by the Moravians (starting in 1849). The Miskitos, however, are culturally distinct and geographically isolated from the Spanish-speaking Honduran population (Clifton Holland, *Latin America and the Caribbean*, World Christianity 4 [Monrovia, Calif.: MARC, 1981], pp. 90-1).

[3]Ibid.

[4]Before we visit our "test course," the evangelical churches in one Tegucigalpa neighborhood, I want to make clear that there are churches in Honduras, and Latin America, very different from the ones in this neighborhood. The next two chapters do not intend to offer a general description of the evangelical church in Latin America. At the same time, what we will see is not unique to this neighborhood. To differing degrees these distortions are present in many churches in Latin America. Evangelical churches have experienced tremendous growth in Latin America over the last twenty to thirty years, and there are many praiseworthy things about evangelicalism in Latin America and the mission efforts that planted these churches. But in our rush to celebrate this success, we must be careful not to overlook significant problems such as those described in the first two chapters.

Chapter 1: Bound Together in Community

[1]"Las Mesetas" is an actual neighborhood, but the name is fictitious.

[2]Almost all Protestant churches in Honduras are evangelical. The term Protestant is not generally used. The Episcopal and Lutheran are the only mainline churches present in Honduras, and their work is quite small in Tegucigalpa and nonexistent in Las Mesetas. Seven of the ten evangelical churches in Las Mesetas are Pentecostal.

[3]Social Scientists such as Christian Lalive d'Epinay have argued that Latin American evangelicals are escapists (Christian Lalive d'Epinay, *The Haven of the Masses* [London: Lutterworth, 1969]). Some political radicals and a few Roman Catholics have also argued that the escapist tendencies of evangelicals in Latin America are the cause for their growth; for example, Enrique Dominguez and Deborah Huntington, "The Salvation Brokers: Conservative Evangelicals in Central America," *NACLA Report on the Americas* 28, no. 1 (1984): 1-36; María Albán Estrada and Juan Pablo Muñoz, *Con Dios todo se puede: La invasión de las sectas al Ecuador* (Quito: Planeta, 1987). It is, however, not only outsiders who make this critique. Some Latin American evangelicals also acknowledge these problems. For example, Adonis Niño Chavarría, "Breve historia del movimiento Pentecostal en Nicaragua," in *Pentecostalismo y liberación: una experiencia latinoamericana*, ed. Carmelo Alvarez (San José, Costa Rica: Departamento Ecuménico de Investigaciones, 1992), p. 50; Pablo Deiros, *Historia del Cristianismo en América*

Latina (Buenos Aires: Fraternidad Teológica Latinoamericana, 1992), pp. 124-25; Samuel Escobar, "Evangelism and Man's Search for Freedom, Justice and Fulfillment," in *Let the Earth Hear His Voice, International Congress on World Evangelization Lausanne, Switzerland, Official Reference Volume: Papers and Responses*, ed. J. D. Douglas (Minneapolis: World Wide Publications, 1975), pp. 305-7; Freddy Guerrero, "Misión y etica social: una perspectiva biblica," *Boletín Teologico* 56 (diciembre 1994): 233-34.

[4]For example, see Judith Chamblis Hoffnagel, "The Believers: Pentecostalism in a Brazilian City" (Ph.D. diss., Indiana University, 1978); Bryan R. Roberts, "Protestant Groups and Coping with Urban Life in Guatemala," *American Journal of Sociology* 73, no. 6 (1968): 753-67; Emilio Willems, *Followers of the New Faith* (Nashville: Vanderbilt University Press, 1967). For overviews of the various interpretations of the growth of evangelicalism in Latin America, see Philip Berryman, "The Coming of Age of Evangelical Protestantism," *NACLA Report on the Americas* 27; no. 6 (1994): 6-10; Samuel Escobar, "Conflict of Interpretations of Popular Protestantism," in *New Face of the Church in Latin America*, ed. Guillermo Cook (Maryknoll, N.Y.: Orbis, 1994), pp. 112-34; David Stoll, "Introduction: Rethinking Protestantism in Latin America," in *Rethinking Protestantism in Latin America*, ed. Virginia Garrard-Burnett and David Stoll (Philadelphia: Temple University Press, 1993), pp. 1-19; Juan Sepulveda, "El crecimiento del movimiento Pentecostal en América Latina," in *Pentecostalismo y liberación: una experiencia latinoamericana*, ed. Carmelo Alvarez (San José, Costa Rica: Departamento Ecuménico de Investigaciones, 1992), pp. 77-88.

[5]These rules and the rules for women's dress are for daily life, not just while in church.

[6]Many social scientists list strict legalism as a characteristic of evangelicals in Latin America. A few scholars have written about the positive concrete impact of these rules in the lives of church members. For instance, Elizabeth Brusco, *The Reformation of Machismo* (Austin: University of Texas Press, 1994); John Burdick, *Looking for God in Brazil: The Progressive Catholic Church in Urban Brazil's Religious Arena* (Berkeley: University of California Press, 1993); Lesley Gill, "'Like a Veil to Cover Them': Women and the Pentecostal Movement in La Paz," *American Ethnologist* 17, no. 4 (1990): 708-21. Some Latin American evangelical theologians who critique the present state of the evangelical church explicitly point to the problem of legalism (René Padilla is an example: C. René Padilla, "Toward a Contextual Christology from Latin America," in *Conflict and Context: Hermeneutics in the Americas*, eds. Mark Lau Branson and C. René Padilla [Grand Rapids, Mich.: Eerdmans, 1986], pp. 90-91); Stanley Slade, a Baptist theologian writing in El Salvador, is the only one I have encountered, however, who investigates explicitly the connection between Latin American evangelicals' legalism and their view of God (Stanley Slade, "Popular Spirituality as an Oppressive Reality," in *New Face of the Church in Latin America*, ed. Guillermo Cook [Maryknoll, N.Y.: Orbis, 1994], pp. 135-49). This book does not seek to contest what he has written, but rather to pursue his observations in a more in-depth way.

[7]I did this ethnographic research in July and August of 1994. I interviewed twenty-four people from ten evangelical churches, did participant observation in three of the churches and interviewed four community leaders. The complete results of the study are published in Mark D. Baker, "Evangelical Churches in a Tegucigalpa Barrio: Do They Fit the Escapist and Legalistic Stereotype? An Ethnographic Investigation," Duke-University of North Carolina Program in Latin American Studies Working Paper 16 (February 1995).

[8]This quote, as well as other quotes and examples that are not credited to someone else,

come from my ethnographic study mentioned in the previous note.

[9]Two examples: "A Christian is someone who does the will of God and obeys and practices what is in the Bible," and "A Christian is someone who not only walks around with a Bible, but someone who by his actions gives testimony to the fact that he is a Christian."

[10]The one exception said, "One needs to know and understand the things of God." If I had worded the question differently, such as, "What does one need to do to accept Jesus as your Savior?" they may have given different answers. I purposefully did not do that because I wanted to see what was foremost in their minds in regard to the issue of becoming an evangelical.

[11]I am currently giving a basic theology class in Amor Fe y Vida Church in Las Mesetas. I had the participants interview neighbors in order to better understand other people's concept of God. The last question they asked people was, "What do you think God will say to you when you die?" The participants had interviewed about thirty people equally divided between evangelicals and nonevangelicals. All of the responses communicated the idea that God would allow them into heaven only if they had been good people.

[12]This woman's understanding is not unique. In Santiago, Chile, David Dixon observed that "evangelicals reported changing their lives of sin to lives of righteousness before they started going to church" (in Stoll, "Introduction: Rethinking Protestantism," p. 4).

[13]Churches present their lists of rules, not as a human list, but as God's commands taken from the Bible. For instance, when I asked one pastor what rules of behavior his church had, he replied, "We do not have any, just those that are stipulated in the Bible." I knew, from talking to former members of his church, that they had a number of very strict rules, including some that are mentioned only indirectly in the Bible and others that are not mentioned at all (such as, no dancing, no wearing shorts for men, no makeup and no going to the movies). Stanley Slade has observed a similar attitude in evangelicals in El Salvador. They have the idea that God only responds to those who pay their dues, so God "only takes care of those who make the sacrifice to attend all the worship services, the vigils and the fasts" (Slade, "Popular Spirituality," p. 138). See also Gill, "'Like a Veil,'" p. 713.

[14]Rubem A. Alves, *Protestantism and Repression: A Brazilian Case Study* (Maryknoll, N.Y.: Orbis, 1985), p. 147.

[15]Apparently, most church members do not think that just because they did not go to church every day they would directly lose their salvation. Rather, they felt they needed to go to church every day so that they would maintain a good relationship with God and so keep from doing things that could cause them to lose their salvation.

[16]This individual is very glad he stopped drinking. He sees that as a good thing, but he will not preach that sermon himself. He wishes they would have preached more about the negativeness of drinking itself. I encountered another example of the use of hell as a deterrant: two teenage sisters were told they had backslidden and were going to hell because they started wearing makeup and earrings.

[17]Elizabeth Brusco's and Lesley Gill's works challenge us to not overlook the positive changes that can happen to men who become believers, both for following these rules and, perhaps most significantly, by not drinking. Brusco and Gill both argue that women allow a certain amount of male domination in Pentecostal churches because they recognize the great benefits women receive by having men involved in the church. The implication is that if the women pushed for more equality in the churches, they might also push the men out. A number of women and men in Las Mesetas did comment on

how the situation in their home had changed for the better when they had become evangelicals. Others, although not denying these positive changes, communicated the need for more improvement in the home.

[18]They cannot afford their own house. She refuses to live with his family, and he refuses to live with hers. So he lives with his mother on one side of the city, and she and the children live with her mother on the other.

[19]This is not to say that all evangelicals only remain at the level of this rule in relation to marriage. Many spoke of significant changes in their relationships.

[20]This is not only an evangelical issue. The Catholic church will not allow couples with only common-law relationships to participate in the Eucharist. Some evangelical churches in Las Mesetas have opened up some space in this area; they will allow people in this category to have minor privileges, such as taking up the offering. One church has taken the step of allowing them to lead singing.

[21]A woman told me of a similar, and quite common, example. She visited a church for six months, but eventually left and has not gone to any other church. She said that they were constantly pushing her to be baptized in the Holy Spirit and speak in tongues. She did not and got tired of being pushed and experiencing the sense of not being part of the "in" group in the church who had spoken in tongues.

[22]Entire churches will go visit others. Most churches, however, do not look positively on individual members visiting another church.

[23]People, however, commented that certain churches were less friendly than others. A number of people said to me, "I always greet them as brother or sister and say 'God bless you,' but I don't sense they are too interested in talking to me, and I wonder if they would greet me, if I did not greet them."

[24]Slade, "Popular Spirituality," p. 137. Because of so much emphasis on threatened punishment it is easy for people to understand salvation as avoiding the wrath of an angry God, rather than being brought into relationship with a loving God. God's love too easily can come to mean restrained anger. Besides the legalistic emphasis that focuses on human behavior, sermons that talk of God in these terms foster this view of God. Yiye Avila, a popular Puerto Rican evangelist who is on the radio in Honduras, preached: "The judgment of God is about to fall upon you. Earthquakes will come, and floods are about to break loose over you. Most humans will perish. All those who are in sin will die and go to hell [pause]. Smile because God loves you! Repent and escape the tragedy that is about to fall upon the earth!" (Sermon in Quito, Ecuador, October 1986, in Estrada and Muñoz, *Con Dios,* p. 66 [translation mine].)

[25]Philip Yancey, *What's So Amazing About Grace?* (Grand Rapids, Mich.: Zondervan, 1997), p. 262.

[26]Yancey, *What's So Amazing,* pp. 14, 15, 33, 203, 263.

Chapter 2: Religion

[1]John Linton, lecture during winter Bible study, January 1984, Oregon Extension of Houghton College, Ashland, Oregon.

[2]My understanding of what I am calling religion has been shaped primarily by the works of Jacques Ellul, including *Living Faith* (San Francisco: Harper & Row, 1983); *Perspectives on Our Age* (New York: Seabury Press, 1981), pp. 85-111; *The Subversion of Christianity* (Grand Rapids, Mich.: Eerdmans, 1986); and *What I Believe* (Grand Rapids, Mich.: Eerdmans, 1989), pp. 3-9. Ellul's discussion of religion obviously stands in relation to Karl Barth's description of religion (Karl Barth, *Church Dogmatics* 1.2

[Edinburgh: T & T Clark, 1956], pp. 280-361).

[3]Ellul gives a variety of examples of religiosity. He states: "The objects of . . . religion may be very different, whether one or more gods projected in heaven, or the Universal. Other dimensions than the human can be apotheosized. Reason can be deified, or science. Hitlerism made its own religion as did Marxism-Leninism up to the late 1970s. The country can be regarded as divine. Progress has become a key term in modern religion. Each cult has its own rites and myths and heretics and believers and raison d'être and believing potential. But the object of religion is not necessarily God" (Ellul, *What I Believe*, pp. 3-4).

[4]Elsa Tamez, *The Amnesty of Grace: Justification by Faith from a Latin American Perspective* (Nashville: Abingdon, 1993), p. 130.

[5]See Jacques Ellul, *The Ethics of Freedom* (Grand Rapids, Mich.: Eerdmans, 1976), p. 152.

[6]Ellul, *Living Faith*, p. 129.

[7]William Stringfellow, *A Private and Public Faith* (Grand Rapids, Mich.: Eerdmans, 1962), p. 17.

[8]Ellul, *Living Faith*, p. 151; *Subversion of Christianity,* pp. 152, 159, 161.

[9]Ellul, *Living Faith*, p. 153. Ellul clarifies: "Speaking of the moment of revelation, I would like to stress that I am not an illuminist or quietist. I'm aware that God's word says something, that the moment has a communicable content, and that God has chosen language so that our words too can get into the game and 'return the serve.' I'm trying to underline the contrast between the living power of revelation and the dead weight of institutional religion" (pp. 153-54).

[10]Stanley Slade, "Popular Spirituality as an Oppressive Reality," in *New Face of the Church in Latin America,* ed. Guillermo Cook (Maryknoll, N.Y.: Orbis, 1994), pp. 138, 139-40.

[11]For a discussion of some of the factors that have influenced Latin Americans' concept of God, see Marcos Baker, "El concepto de Dios en America Latina," *Boletín Teológico: Revista de la Fraternidad Teológica Latinoamericana* 28 no. 61 (1996): 39-55. For a shorter version in English see Mark David Baker, "Freedom from Legalism and Freedom for Community: A Hermeneutical Case Study of Reading Galatians in a Tegucigalpa Barrio," (Ph.D. diss., Duke University, Durham, N.C., 1996), pp. 122-27.

[12]Doug Frank, "Straitened & Narrowed," *Books & Culture: A Christian Review* 3, no. 6 (1997): 27.

[13]The song "Oh Be Careful" is by Alfred B. Smith and is in the public domain.

[14]Frank, "Straitened & Narrowed," p. 27.

[15]See, for instance, the following works by Doug Frank, "Straitened & Narrowed"; "Seeing Jesus," *The Crucible: A Journal for Christian Graduate Students* 3, no. 2 (1993): 20-2; and especially "The Strangely Distant God of American Evangelicals," Lectures at the McKenzie Study Center, Eugene, Ore., October 2-3, 1992.

[16]Doug Frank, "Remarks for the Third Re-Forming the Center Conference," Messiah College, June 1, 1996, p. 1.

[17]Frank, "Straitened & Narrowed," p. 27.

[18]Justo L. González, *Y hasta lo último de la tierra: Una historia ilustrada del cristianismo,* vol. 7, *La era de los conquistadores* (Miami: Caribe, 1980), pp. 215-16.

[19]This is just one of the many significant ways that the Spanish conquest, when the cross and sword invaded Latin America together, has affected the Christianity that is practiced today in Latin America. For a more complete discussion see Baker, "Freedom from Legalism," pp. 86-92, 111-17, 124-25; and Baker, "El concepto de Dios," pp. 40-46.

[20]The most famous example is the Virgin of Guadalupe in Mexico. The shrine to her is on the same hill that had been a sanctuary dedicated to Tonantzin ("Our Mother"), the fertility goddess of the Aztecs.

[21]This is not say that there are not practicing Catholics in Latin America who have experienced true conversion to Christianity. Also, the evaluation and critique found in this section is not as negative as it is simply because it is written by an evangelical. For instance, Enrique Dussel, a leading Latin American historian and Catholic liberation theologian, has made similar evaluations. He emphasizes that although typical Latin Americans call themselves "Catholics" because they were baptized, this does not mean they are truly Christian (Enrique Dussel, *A History of the Church in Latin America* [Grand Rapids, Mich.: Eerdmans, 1981], see especially pp. 68-71, 117-20).

[22]This is a generalization, and there are exceptions. For instance, missionary authors such as John Mackay and Stanley Rycroft recognized the need to challenge, in more than superficial ways, the religion present in Latin America (John Mackay, *The Other Spanish Christ* [New York: Macmillan, 1933]; W. Stanley Rycroft, *Religion and Faith in Latin America* [Philadelphia: Westminster Press, 1958].

[23]In fact, religious bargaining with God is at times explicitly encouraged in evangelical churches. A preacher in Las Mesetas told his listeners that if they hoped to receive anything from God, they must first obey what God says (a sermon in the Príncipe de Paz church, Las Mesetas, July 3, 1994). A preacher in Brazil told his congregation that they must demonstrate their faith by giving to God. He asked them to demonstrate their faith by giving to the church and told them that God would respond by giving them a job. (Paul Pretiz heard this sermon at the Brazilian Igreja Universal del Reino de Deus. Paul Pretiz, interview by author, San José, Costa Rica, July 12, 1995.)

[24]See Slade, "Popular Spirituality," pp. 135-49.

[25]I recall, while evangelizing as a teenager, being concerned about whether the person I had just evangelized had, in fact, become a Christian because they left out part of the prayer I had told them to pray.

[26]Others stress that feelings are not significant. See, for example, "The Four Spiritual Laws" (San Bernardino, Calif.: Campus Crusade for Christ, 1965), now titled "Would You Like to Know God Personally?" (Orlando, Fla.: New Life/Campus Crusade for Christ, n.d.).

[27]I do not mean to imply that Catholicism is by definition religious. Rather, the popular religiosity of the pilgrim mentioned is often a religious subversion of orthodox Catholicism, just as many practices of evangelicals are subversions of orthodox Protestantism. For a more complete discussion of the difference between popular Catholicism and orthodox Catholicism in Latin America, see Pablo Deiros, *Historia del Cristianismo en América Latina* (Buenos Aires: Fraternidad Teológica Latinoamericana, 1992), pp. 147-57.

[28]Rowan Williams, *A Ray of Darkness: Sermons and Reflections* (Boston: Cowley, 1995), p. 193.

[29]Ibid.

[30]Ibid.

[31]Tilden H. Edwards, *Spiritual Friend* (New York: Paulist, 1980), p. 15.

Chapter 3: Rejecting Counterfeit Community

[1]This name and the others in this chapter are fictitious.

[2]Amor Fe y Vida Church does not have a paid pastor.

[3]John Knox Presbyterian Church hoped to work in partnership with the evangelical churches in Las Mesetas to improve the living conditions there. The local churches, however, were not as interested, and some did not see this as part of their ministry. After a number of years of trying, John Knox Presbyterian ended up working more closely with a small Honduran development agency. Through this agency, they loaned residents in Las Mesetas money to build houses and start small businesses.

[4]Clearly the Christians in Amor Fe y Vida Church experienced both a lack of and resistance to a holistic gospel in other churches in Las Mesetas. The level of escapism in the other churches, however, varies, and evaluating their apparent social passivity is complex. An emphasis on individual salvation and individual morality does have social consequences. Yet, with those from Amor Fe y Vida, we could ask how much more could be happening if these other churches preached and lived a holistic gospel. For a detailed discussion of the "escapism" and social involvement of the churches in Las Mesetas see Mark D. Baker, "Evangelical Churches in a Tegucigalpa Barrio: Do They Fit the Escapist and Legalistic Stereotype? An Ethnographic Investigation," Duke-University of North Carolina Program in Latin American Studies Working Paper 16 (February 1995). See also the study by John Burdick where, in the context of a small Brazilian city, he demonstrates that Pentecostals in some ways contribute more toward social change than a base community of the Catholic Church (John Burdick, *Looking for God in Brazil: The Progressive Catholic Church in Urban Brazil's Religious Arena* [Berkeley: University of California Press, 1993]).

[5]For instance, although they may be related in Las Mesetas, these two are not always present together. Some churches can be quite "legalistic" about helping the poor or other forms of social activism.

Chapter 4: Religion Produces Individualistic-Spiritualized Christianity
[1]Washington Padilla saw a similar use of a spiritualizing lens by the evangelicals in Ecuador. He states, "[conservative fundamentalism in Ecuador] never has understood, for example, what the New Testament means to say with terms like 'this world' and 'this age,' and therefore has reduced them to individualistic terms, to personal problems and vices, instead of taking note that they refer to a total social, economic, and political system of evil and injustices that has victims which the church is called to help, heal, and redeem in a holistic manner; nor has it fully understood its mission for similar reasons, because it has not understood, for example the meaning of the kingdom of God and its justice and conservative fundamentalism has reduced it and understood it in individualistic and spiritual terms" (Washington Padilla, *La iglesia y los Dioses modernos: historia del protestantismo en el Ecuador* [Quito: Corporación Editora Nacional, 1989], pp. 427-28 [translation mine]).

[2]Ken Morris led me to see the significance of this lens in relation to these issues (Ken Morris, "Evangelicalism and Christocentric Universalism: Past Roots, Present Manifestations and Future Implications" [M.A. thesis, New College Berkeley, 1988]. René Padilla uses a similar metaphor: "The individualism of 'culture Christianity' . . . sees the Lord with only one eye, as an individualistic Jesus who is concerned with the salvation of individuals" (C. René Padilla, *Mission Between the Times* [Grand Rapids, Mich.: Eerdmans, 1985], p. 22).

[3]Jacques Ellul, *The Subversion of Christianity* (Grand Rapids, Mich.: Eerdmans, 1986), p. 8.

[4]Dennis P. Hollinger, *Individualism and Social Ethics: An Evangelical Syncretism* (Lanham,

Md.: University Press of America, 1983), pp. 13-18, 44. For a discussion of the sources of individualism, specifically focused on individualism and evangelicalism, see Hollinger, *Individualism*, pp. 19-38; George M. Marsden, *The Evangelical Mind and the New School Presbyterian Experience* (New Haven: Yale University Press, 1970), pp. 235-39; and Dennis Voskuil, "Individualism and Evangelism in America," *Reformed Review* 41 (autumn 1987): 21-28. In "Another Look at the American Character" Emmet Fields emphasizes the importance of recognizing other strands in the American character besides individualism; in the end he concludes, "The sensible view is to see liberty and individualism intertwined with equality and conformity throughout American History, deep in the character of all of us even though we lean one way or the other personally" (*Soundings* 65 [spring 1982]: 56).

[5]Hollinger, *Individualism*, pp. 16-17.

[6]Ibid., pp. 18, 44.

[7]Ibid., p. 44.

[8]Stephen Hart, "Privatization in American Religion and Society," *Sociological Analysis* 47 (winter 1987): 325.

[9]Alan Carter offers a helpful discussion of differences between individualism and collectivism in "On Individualism, Collectivism, and Interrelationism," *Heythrop Journal* 31 (January 1990): 23-38.

[10]Nor is the point that having a more collectivist approach in and of itself will correct the problems we observed, as Stephen Fowl and Gregory Jones (*Reading in Communion* [Grand Rapids, Mich.: Eerdmans, 1991], p. 64) observe. "To be sure, there are some communities that are doing a remarkable job of socializing their members. Unfortunately, the character of the people socialized in these contexts often reflects corrupted conceptions of Christian life."

[11]The class was at Duke Divinity School during the fall semester 1992. Hays discusses the corporate versus individualistic reading of Rom 12:1 in Richard B. Hays, *The Moral Vision of the New Testament* (San Francisco: Harper, 1996), pp. 35-36.

[12]C. Norman Kraus, *The Community of the Spirit* (Scottdale, Penn.: Herald Press, 1993), p. 32.

[13]Ibid., p. 43.

[14]Ibid., p. 56.

[15]Rodney Clapp, *A Peculiar People: The Church as Culture in a Post-Christian Society* (Downers Grove, Ill.: InterVarsity Press, 1996), p. 91.

[16]Ibid., pp. 91-92.

[17]Kraus, *Community of the Spirit*, pp. 53-54. For a more complete development of this theme, see Kraus's chapter "The Individual-in-Community in the Bible," pp. 31-56.

[18]See Clapp, *Peculiar People*, especially chapters 2, 4.

[19]To define evangelicalism in the United States is no easy task. It is helpful to think of evangelicalism as a specific movement that sought to reform fundamentalism from within—those who identified with the National Association of Evangelicals, which was formed in 1942. This may, however, make too great a distinction between fundamentalists and evangelicals. This book does not seek to emphasize this distinction. One reason is that many nonevangelicals use the term *fundamentalist* in a broad way that includes many evangelicals who would not call themselves fundamentalists. At times I use the term *fundamentalist* when referring specifically to Christians who would have used that term for themselves earlier in this century. In general, the term *evangelical* will refer to a movement that includes proto-fundamentalists in the late nineteenth

century, fundamentalists in the early twentieth century and those called evangelicals and fundamentalists today.

[20]This list taken from George Marsden, *Fundamentalism and American Culture* (New York: Oxford University Press, 1980), pp. 82-83. For further examples, see Donald Dayton, *Discovering an Evangelical Heritage* (New York: Harper & Row, 1976); Donald Dayton, "Pentecostal/Charismatic Renewal and Social Change: A Western Perspective," *Transformation* 5, no. 4 (1988): 7-9. Marsden explains that this social concern or social action took two forms. One approach was to use "political means to promote the welfare of society, especially of the poor and oppressed." The second relied on private charity to meet such needs. "Before the Civil War many evangelicals displayed neither type of social concern, many others emphasized both." From 1865-1900 the political expression of social concern lessened, but the expressions of private charity remained strong (p. 86).

[21]David O. Moberg, *The Great Reversal: Evangelism Versus Social Concern* (Philadelphia: Lippincott, 1972), p. 32.

[22]Moberg, *Great Reversal*, pp. 30-31. For further examples, see Donald Dayton, "The Social and Political Conservatism of Modern American Evangelicalism: A Preliminary Search for the Reasons," *Union Seminary Quarterly Review* 32, no. 2 (1977): 70-71.

[23]This is not to deny the social consequences of the Christianity brought from the North. A potential problem of those who stress the importance of the "Great Reversal" is to ignore the social significance of even the spiritualized gospel. As I noted in chapter one, Elizabeth Brusco, John Burdick, Lesley Gill and others have noted the significant consequences of the evangelical emphasis on not drinking—even if communicated in the context of an individualistic-spiritualized gospel. Dayton also cautions against too quickly dismissing the social impact of Pentecostals just because they are not involved in what is commonly thought of as social action (Dayton, "Pentecostal/Charismatic Renewal," p. 11). The point of this section, and of this book, is not to downplay the importance of individual salvation, but rather to point out how truncated the gospel preached in a place like Las Mesetas is, because it emphasizes only the individual-spiritual side of salvation.

[24]For a discussion of the causes, see Dayton, *Discovering an Evangelical Heritage*, pp. 121-37; Dayton, "Pentecostal/Charismatic Renewal," pp. 7-9; Dayton, "Social and Political Conservatism," pp. 71-80; Marsden, *Fundamentalism*, pp. 85-93; Moberg, *Great Reversal*, pp. 28-43.

[25]For an in-depth study of this shift from postmillennialism to premillennialism, see Douglas W. Frank, *Less Than Conquerors: How Evangelicals Entered the Twentieth Century* (Grand Rapids, Mich.: Eerdmans, 1986), especially chapters two and three.

[26]Dwight L. Moody, cited in C. Norman Kraus, *An Intrusive Gospel?* (Downers Grove, Ill.: InterVarsity Press, 1998), p. 13.

[27]Dayton, "Social and Political Conservatism," p. 77. "Premillennial mission theorists of the late nineteenth century believed that they were living in the last days before Christ's return. The implication for mission theory of their 'end-time' hopes was a single-minded emphasis on evangelization. Proclamation of the gospel took precedence over such traditional missionary activity as education and medicine" (Dana L. Robert, "'The Crisis of Missions': Premillennial Mission Theory and the Origins of Independent Evangelical Missions," in *Earthen Vessels: American Evangelicals and Foreign Missions, 1880-1980*, eds. Joel A. Carpenter and Wilbert Shenk [Grand Rapids, Mich.: Eerdmans, 1990], p. 32).

[28]Marsden, *Fundamentalism*, pp. 91-92; Moberg, *Great Reversal*, pp. 34-35.

[29]René Padilla laments that the "Great Reversal" coincided with a huge increase in missionary activity. "For this reason many of the churches that the modern missionary movement started in Latin America and on other continents were born with a very limited vision of Christian mission" (C. René Padilla, "La Fraternidad Teológica Latinoamericana y la responsabilidad social de la iglesia," *Boletín Teológico* 59-60 [1995]: 100).

[30]In 1956 a writer in *Christianity Today* still saw the need to battle the social gospel. Addison Leitch wrote, "There is no salvation by way of the social gospel, but only in the individual's call to Christ" (cited in Hollinger, *Individualism*, p. 99). In many ways the "Great Reversal" has continued to this day. René Padilla describes efforts by the United States missionary establishment in the 1980s to roll back, or at least limit, the steps taken toward embracing a holistic gospel at Lausanne (Padilla, "La Fraternidad Teológica Latinoamericana," pp. 101-2). Most evangelicals, however, who more recently lived out, and live out, a Christianity that was rather indifferent to social problems did not do so as a direct reaction against liberalism. Rather, the "Great Reversal" had been lived out so long that it had become standard practice.

[31]The King James Version, Revised Standard Version, New American Standard Bible, New International Version and Today's English Version all have similar translations.

[32]This literal translation is taken from *The Greek-English New Testament* published and distributed by *Christianity Today* (Washington D.C.: Christianity Today, 1977), p. 531. I have purposefully used a literal translation published by an evangelical institution to emphasize the point that the argument is not about the literal translation of the verse but about how one puts it into meaningful English. I have left out the words this literal translation adds in brackets—[is] and [he is].

[33]For a discussion of the translation of this verse, see Victor Paul Furnish, *2 Corinthians*, Anchor Bible Commentary (Garden City, N.Y.: Doubleday, 1984), pp. 332-33; and Ralph P. Martin, *2 Corinthians*, Word Biblical Commentary (Waco, Tex.: Word, 1986), p. 152. Both Furnish and Martin use "there is a new creation" in their translations.

[34]Joel Green, "America's Bible: Good News for All Nations?" *Radix* 18, no. 4: 26. See also Hays, *Moral Vision*, p. 20.

[35]This is not to say that there were not other influences within the framework of the missionaries that helped produce these characteristics. For instance, they also inherited problems from Greek thought that the church has battled since its early days, such as a docetic Christology and a preoccupation with a spiritual soul rather than the body.

[36]Marsden, *Fundamentalism*, p. 71. In 1908 E. Y. Mullins, president of Southern Baptist Theological Seminary, wrote, "Religion is a personal matter between the soul and God." (From Mullins's *The Axioms of Religion*, cited in Harold Bloom, *The American Religion: The Emergence of the Post-Christian Nation* [New York: Simon & Schuster, 1992], p. 227.) The continuing importance of this idea is demonstrated by the fact that a revised version of Mullins's *The Axioms of Religion* was published in 1978 by Broadman Press.

[37]John Woodbridge, Mark A. Noll, Nathan O. Hatch, *The Gospel in America: Themes in the Story of America's Evangelicals* (Grand Rapids, Mich.: Zondervan, 1979), p. 175. Marsden sums it up saying, "The church was essentially a collection of converted individuals" (Marsden, *Reforming Fundamentalism* [Grand Rapids, Mich.: Eerdmans, 1987], p. 29 [see also p. 4]).

[38]Marsden, *Fundamentalism*, p. 37. Hollinger writes: "[Evangelicals] view the degenerate proclivity of society as resulting from the accumulation of individual sins. There has

been little conception of corporate or structural sin among evangelicals—at least not until the 1970s. This phenomenon is a natural corollary to their atomistic view of society" (Hollinger, *Individualism,* p. 132).

[39]Marsden, *Fundamentalism,* p. 37. In 1966 at the third annual Lutheran Free Conference, Rev. Norman W. Berg stated that the mission of the church is the salvation of souls, not the redemption of society; the latter will be a "natural byproduct of the preaching of the gospel" (Moberg, *Great Reversal,* p. 89). In 1964 J. Howard Pew wrote in *Christianity Today,* "The mission of the church is to redeem souls by the gospel of salvation, and only as she redeems individuals will society be redeemed" (cited in Hollinger, *Individualism,* p. 100). In a 1976 interview in *Christianity Today* Bill Bright was asked, "If we had, say 400 people of God in Congress, could we expect things to be any different from they are now?" Bright responded, "About 1,000 percent different." As Hollinger observes, "Such a statement presupposes many things, but among them is the view that social structures are nothing more than the people comprising them. Change the people and the corporate realities will necessarily be changed" (Hollinger, *Individualism,* p. 130). Hollinger gives numerous similar quotes from the pages of *Christianity Today* from 1956-1976 (Hollinger, *Individualism,* pp. 94-101, 126-30). It would not be insignificant to have 400 people in Congress practicing the personal morality that Bright would have stressed. The instruction in individualistic morality that Bright would have given them, however, would not lead them to address structural issues of justice. In fact, it can allow Christians to participate directly in structural injustice even while perceiving themselves as dedicated Christians. John P. Crozier is an excellent mid-nineteenth century example of this. He donated time and money to religious causes; he was interested in the moral reform of his life and that of his workers; he visited sick workers; and in his old age he donated much of his wealth made in cotton mills. He also, however, "fired workers who reacted to cruel wage cuts by daring to organize strikes," and he broke labor laws. "In his own church he always insisted that pastors 'confine themselves to strictly biblical themes, and to the achievement of distinctly spiritual results,' for he maintained that evangelism was ultimately the only answer to this world's ills" (Frank, *Less Than Conquerors,* p. 36). See also William Stringfellow, *A Private and Public Faith* (Grand Rapids, Mich.: Eerdmans, 1962), p. 28.

[40]Samuel Escobar, "Heredero de la reforma radical," in *Hacia una teología evangélica latinoamericana,* ed. C. René Padilla (Miami: Caribe, 1984), p. 60 (translation mine). René Padilla states that a focus on numerical growth increases the use of the gospel package. He writes, "Evangelism becomes a technique to 'win souls,' and for this, theological reflection is unnecessary; it is enough to use canned methods and imported formulas of salvation" (Padilla, *Mission Between the Times,* p. 101). Translating Christian truth into propositions, rules and principles also springs from an atmosphere of modern rationality and Christians' desire to base their faith on facts and certainty.

[41]Since the Bible is mostly narrative, it would be more biblical to put more emphasis on a narrative form, rather than propositional, when we are attempting to communicate the truth of Christianity. See N. T. Wright, "How Can the Bible Be Authoritative?" *Vox Evangelica* 21 (1991): 7-32.

[42]I do not claim to have a place outside of culture that allows me to see a "pure" biblical truth and hence judge the truth in the package as lacking. In fact that is the kind of attitude that has produced the gospel package and left those who travel with such packages blind to how deeply their own culture shapes the package they carry.

[43]C. René Padilla, "Hermeneutics and Culture: A Theological Perspective," in *Down to*

Earth: Studies in Christianity and Culture, The Papers of The Lausanne Consultation on Gospel and Culture, eds. Robert T. Coote and John Stott (Grand Rapids, Mich.: Eerdmans, 1980), p. 78; see also Padilla, *Mission Between the Times,* p. 85.

[44]The woman was from the Las Mesetas Iglesia de Dios de la Profecía (Church of God of Prophecy). The tract was printed by the denomination of the same name centered in Cleveland, Tennessee.

[45]Padilla, "Hermeneutics and Culture," p. 77.

[46]Plutarco Bonilla, "Crisis del protestantismo costarricense actual," *Pastoralia* 9, no. 18 (1987): 67, 90.

Chapter 5: The Traditional Reading of Galatians

[1]I do not mean to imply that all evangelicals hold to the traditional interpretation. I will cite a number of evangelical authors in the following chapters who, in a variety of ways, differ with this traditional view. What is described in this section has been, and still is, the most common interpretation in evangelical circles. Among the works this section is based on are F. F. Bruce, *The Epistle to the Galatians: A Commentary on the Greek Text,* New International Greek Testament Commentary (Grand Rapids, Mich.: Eerdmans, 1982); Charles H. Cosgrove, "Galatians," in *Mercer Commentary on the Bible,* eds. Watson Mills and Richard Wilson (Macon, Ga.: Mercer University Press, 1995), pp. 1207-15; E. F. Harrison, "Galatians," in *The Wycliffe Bible Commentary,* eds. C. F. Pfeiffer and E. F. Harrison (Chicago: Moody Press, 1962), pp. 1283-99; Harold Lindsell, ed., *Harper Study Bible* (Grand Rapids, Mich.: Zondervan, 1982), pp. 1736-45; Samuel J. Mikolaski, "Galatians," in *The New Bible Commentary: Revised,* eds. D. Guthrie and J. A. Motyer, (London: Inter-Varsity Press, 1970), pp. 1089-1104; Leon Morris, *Galatians: Paul's Charter of Christian Freedom* (Downers Grove, Ill.: InterVarsity Press, 1996); Charles C. Ryrie, *The Ryrie Study Bible* (Chicago: Moody Press, 1978); Ray C. Stedman, sermon, "Galatians: Don't Submit Again to the Slave's Yoke," Peninsula Bible Church, Palo Alto, Calif., Sept. 17, 1967; Merrill Tenney, *The Charter of Christian Liberty* (Grand Rapids, Mich.: Eerdmans, 1968).

[2]Harrison, "Galatians," p. 1283.

[3]Some explicitly discuss the theme of Galatians in terms of the individual (Mikolaski, "Galatians," p. 1091; Ryrie, *Ryrie Study Bible,* p. 1769; Tenney, *Charter of Christian Liberty,* p. 27); others use terms such as "the spiritual welfare of the Galatian Christians" or "believers," which in the context of their writing, which lacks any corporate emphasis, gives the impression that Paul is focusing on the issue of individual salvation (Lindsell, *Harper Study Bible,* p. 1736).

[4]For example, Harrison, "Galatians," p. 1284; Mikolaski, "Galatians," p. 1092.

[5]Harrison, "Galatians," p. 1288; Mikolaski, "Galatians," p. 1095.

[6]The individualistic emphasis is evident, for example, when Harrison states, "one can become just in God's sight only by faith. On this basis alone can he truly live the life of God" (in reference to 3:11-12) (Harrison, "Galatians," p. 1291).

[7]Tenney, *Charter of Christian Liberty,* p.118; see also Morris, *Galatians: Paul's Charter,* p. 86.

[8]Harrison, "Galatians," p. 1290. Ryrie's definition is "to be declared righteous in God's sight and to be vindicated of any charge of sin in connection with failure to keep God's law" (Ryrie, *Ryrie Study Bible,* p. 1772).

[9]Mikolaski, "Galatians," p. 1096.

[10]Harrison, "Galatians," p. 1296; Mikolaski, "Galatians," p. 1097.

[11]Morris, *Galatians: Paul's Charter,* p. 189; Mikolaski, "Galatians," p. 1104; Charles Cosgrove, however, does not give an individualistic reading; he writes, "the community of those in Christ is the locus of the new creation" (Cosgrove, "Galatians," p. 1215).

[12]In a sense I am following the standard approach of modern biblical scholarship, which focuses on what Paul meant and cautions against too quickly jumping to a discussion of what a text means for us today. At the same time, I obviously begin the study with a certain agenda—things I hope to find. I do not pretend to present a neutral reading of Paul. As I stated in the introduction, things I observed in Las Mesetas prompted my study of Galatians. An experience in a particular context led me to reflect on how a particular text might relate in a helpful way to that context. To begin the following chapter with the appearance of coming to the text with certain neutrality would be an illusion. Of course, in reality the idea to study Galatians in relation to the problems observed in Las Mesetas could not have started in Las Mesetas. I had to have a notion of what Galatians was about in order to think it had something to say to Las Mesetas. This just further points to the interactive nature of biblical hermeneutics. One cannot so easily put either the text or the context as starting points.

Chapter 6: The Problem in Galatia

[1]Contrast, for instance, Romans 1:8; 1 Corinthians 1:4; Philippians 1:3.

[2]The most explicit references to these other teachers are 1:6-9; 3:1-2; 4:17; 5:7-12; 6:12-14. An exact description of these teachers and their motivations is not possible. We cannot even be sure they are outsiders. Apparently they are Jews (6:13), but it is possible they were Gentiles attempting to gain favor, to prove themselves, with Jewish Christians who also held to this teaching. J. Louis Martyn argues that they represent a law-observant mission to the Gentiles and "are in the full sense of the term evangelists, finding their basic identity not as persons who struggle against Paul, but rather as those who preach God's good news" (J. Louis Martyn, "A Law-Observant-Mission to the Gentiles," *Scottish Journal of Theology* 38 [1985]: 314).

[3]Scot McKnight, *Galatians,* The NIV Application Commentary (Grand Rapids, Mich.: Zondervan, 1995), p. 28.

[4]In my opinion, the "Lord's Supper" in the early church was not a separate cultic event, but was "an entire ordinary meal" that a Christian community may have eaten each time they came together. (Robert Banks, *Paul's Idea of Community,* rev. ed., [Peabody, Mass.: Hendrickson, 1994], p. 81; see also R. Allen Cole, *Galatians,* 2nd ed., Tyndale New Testament Commentary [Grand Rapids, Mich.: Eerdmans, 1989], pp. 115-16.) Philip F. Esler prefers to distinguish between table-fellowship and Eucharistic table-fellowship "where those present shared, that is to say, actually passed around from hand to hand, one loaf of bread and one cup of wine" (Philip F. Esler, *The First Christians in Their Social Worlds: Social Scientific Approaches to New Testament Interpretation* [London: Routledge, 1994], p. 52). Banks reports that breaking bread in this way and sharing a cup at the end of the meal, both accompanied by prayers of blessing, was not "different from the customary meal for guests in a Jewish home" (Banks, *Paul's Idea of Community,* p. 81). In either case, both Banks and Esler agree that the Eucharist was a meal the church ate together and it "was the most tangible expression of the unity in Jesus Christ of Jew and Greek, slave and free, male and female (Gal 3:28)" (Esler, *First Christians,* p. 53; see Banks, *Paul's Idea of Community,* p. 83).

[5]J. Gresham Machen, *Machen's Notes on Galatians,* ed. John Skilton (Philadelphia: Presbyterian & Reformed, 1973), pp. 143-44. These "notes" were originally published

as a series of articles in the earlier *Christianity Today* from January 1931 to February 1933.

[6]For example, see F. F. Bruce, *The Epistle to the Galatians: A Commentary on the Greek Text*, NIGTC (Grand Rapids, Mich.: Eerdmans, 1982), p. 131. Others who, like Machen, make no mention of the issue of unity include Charles Erdman, *The Epistle of Paul to the Galatians* (Philadelphia: Westminster Press, 1930), pp. 7-11, 47-52; and Harold Lindsell, ed., *Harper Study Bible* (Grand Rapids, Mich.: Zondervan, 1982), p. 1739.

[7]Hansen writes: "Peter's separation from table fellowship with Gentile Christians implied that salvation for Gentiles required strict adherence to the law and incorporation into the Jewish nation. . . . Since the consequences and implications of Peter's action were so destructive to the unity and spiritual integrity of the church, Paul had no choice but to confront Peter. . . . Peter's separation had violated his own conviction that the racial division between Jews and Gentiles should not exist in the church" (G. Walter Hansen, *Galatians*, IVP New Testament Commentary [Downers Grove, Ill.: InterVarsity Press, 1994], pp. 66-67).

[8]Ibid., p. 14; see also G. Walter Hansen, "Galatians, Letter to the," in *Dictionary of Paul and His Letters*, ed. Gerald Hawthorne, Ralph P. Martin and Daniel G. Reid (Downers Grove, Ill.: InterVarsity Press, 1993), pp. 323-34. Although they do not do so as forcefully as Hansen, fellow evangelicals Scot McKnight and Moisés Silva place the letter within the context of division caused by Judaizers trying to force Gentile Christians to become Jews (McKnight, *Galatians*, pp. 19-47; Moisés Silva, "Galatians," in *New Bible Commentary: 21st Century Edition*, eds. D. A. Carson, J. Motyer and R. T. France [Downers Grove, Ill.: InterVarsity Press, 1994], p. 1206).

[9]Hansen, *Galatians*, pp. 67-8. Hansen is not the first to argue for a more social reading of Galatians. Many have followed the lead of Markus Barth and Krister Stendahl who emphasized the social character of justification in Paul's writings. See Markus Barth, "The Kerygma of Galatians," *Interpretation* 21 (April 1967): 131-46; Markus Barth, "Jews and Gentiles: The Social Character of Justification in Paul," *Journal of Ecumenical Studies* 5 (1968): 241-67; Krister Stendahl, *Paul Among Jews and Gentiles* (Philadelphia: Fortress, 1976). Hansen is used as an example because, like the other authors in this section, he is an evangelical.

[10]E. P. Sanders, *Paul and Palestinian Judaism* (Philadelphia: Fortress, 1977), pp. 180, 419-28.

[11]Elsa Tamez offers a similar critique of Sanders. She states that "Sanders' word of caution is important, but it cannot mask the fact that Paul's affirmation in Galatians that one is justified by faith and not by works of the law points toward an important truth about human existence: To live in Christ is to live in freedom, while to submit oneself to the law is to return to a condition of slavery" (Elsa Tamez, *The Amnesty of Grace: Justification by Faith from a Latin American Perspective* [Nashville: Abingdon, 1993], pp. 76-77). Tamez, writing in Latin America, is less haunted by the issue of Israel and anti-Semitism that marks the work of so many European and North American postwar Pauline scholars. She obviously considers other issues more pressing for Latin America. Although some may critique her work, Segundo's (see the next section), or mine as potentially fostering anti-Semitism, that comment would reflect a superficial reading. We all point to deeper and more universal problems than Judaism itself. In the following section, I will argue that Paul makes a similar move in Galatians 4:3-11. Chapter two of this book demonstrates that evangelicalism, my tradition, can be just as enslaving as the law Tamez mentions in the above quote.

R. H. Gundry offers a critique of Sanders that, although significantly different from mine, shares some similarities because it emphasizes that, in relation to "staying in," the way Paul discusses ethical issues differs significantly from Judaism. It is not just that Paul offers a different set of rules, but that the whole discussion is in a different key. "Though obedience is integral and important to Paul's theology, alongside Palestinian Jewish absorption in legal questions his comments on obedience look proportionately slight. Furthermore they usually take the form of exhortations, not of legal interpretation, extension, and application" (R. H. Gundry, "Grace, Works, and Staying Saved in Paul," *Biblica* 66 [1985]: 7). This demonstrates that Gundry has more sensitivity than Sanders does to the issue of not just what is said, but how it is said and how much it is said. Although I agree with Gundry's critique of Sanders on this point, Gundry may be wrong to limit Paul's concern in Galatia to the issue of "staying in." In real life, the distinction between getting in and staying in may not be so clear. If the false teachers could lead the people to think they must be circumcised to stay in, it is easy to imagine that some Gentile Christians, or especially new converts, could come to see it as a requirement for getting in. Therefore, Paul might very well have been concerned about the implications their teaching had for people's understanding of "getting in" as well. (Gundry, "Grace, Works," pp. 1-38).

[12]Although the Jewish writings may make mention of God's grace, their overwhelming focus on presenting and discussing rules for human behavior allows them to become rich soil for religion. When seized by religion, these rules become potential sources of works-righteousness. Sanders himself acknowledges that God's saving action through the covenant is "more presupposed than directly discussed" (Sanders, *Paul and Palestinian Judaism*, p. 236).

[13]Sanders states that Paul's "criticism of his native religion has nothing to do with whether or not some are inclined toward self-righteousness. . . . When he criticizes Judaism, he does so in a sweeping manner, and the criticism has two focuses: the lack of faith in Christ and the lack of equality for the Gentiles." Sanders argues that the dispute in Galatians is not about "doing" as such. It is not a conflict between "doing" and "faith." He maintains that both sides had requirements, and to have requirements is not to deny the importance of faith (E. P. Sanders, *Paul, the Law and the Jewish People* [Philadelphia: Fortress, 1983], pp. 155, 157, 159).

[14]Ironically, the above paragraph uses Sanders's work to warn us against doing what I have accused him of doing—of placing too much emphasis on "official" teaching and ignoring the power of religion.

[15]Of course, Paul himself, in the letter to the Galatians, offers ethical direction, but the ethical section of Galatians is less easily seized and turned into religion. It is preceded not just by a brief statement mentioning God's grace but by almost five full chapters that emphasize the centrality of God's gracious action in salvation. Also Paul's imperatives are not the type that so easily lend themselves to clear measurement and differentiation between those who follow them and those who do not. That is necessary for religious application of ethical imperatives. For further discussion of this see chapter nine.

[16]We cannot know for sure what lies behind the threatened persecution. Philip Esler, however, offers an account that meshes well with the "religious" reading I have proposed. He gives this summary: "(a) Paul's opponents in Galatia, Jewish Christians themselves threatened with persecution by non-Christian Jews, were concerned at some aspect of the association between Jews and Gentiles in the local Christian communities.

(b) So seriously did his opponents in Galatia regard the situation that they were encouraging the Gentile members of their communities to be circumcised. (c) The Jewish Christians may have been threatening to end their association with the Gentiles unless they were to be circumcised and keep the Law" (Esler, *First Christians*, p. 61).

[17]An inclusive reading of "we" is more common, but some, Bruce for instance, opt for an exclusive Jewish "we" (Bruce, *Epistle to the Galatians*, p. 193; For further discussion of this translation issue, see Richard Longenecker, *Galatians*, WBC [Dallas: Word, 1990], p. 164; J. Louis Martyn, *Galatians*, Anchor Bible [New York: Doubleday, 1997], pp. 334-36, 393). An inclusive "we" places both Jew and Gentile in common enslavement in this one verse. An exclusive "we" emphasizes specifically that the Jews were enslaved and then read in conjunction with 4:8-9 demonstrates a common enslavement with Gentiles.

[18]Bruce, *Epistle to the Galatians*, p. 193; Longenecker, *Galatians*, p. 165; Martyn, *Galatians*, pp. 393-406.

[19]Bruce, *Epistle to the Galatians*, p. 193.

[20]Peter T. O'Brien, *Colossians, Philemon*, Word Biblical Commentary (Waco, Tex.: Word, 1982), p. 132.

[21]Bruce (*Epistle to the Galatians*, p. 191), and Dunn opt for this translation (James D. G. Dunn, *A Commentary on the Epistle to the Galatians* [London: A. C. Black, 1993], pp. 212-13).

[22]Using the word *power* naturally brings up the question of the Pauline language of powers and principalities. Although I believe that *stoicheia* belongs within a discussion of Paul's concept of principalities and powers, and although I believe that Paul would approve of including "religion" as one of the principalities and powers, I will not argue those points in this book. It would require not only argument on why *stoicheia* is included, but also significant discussion of what Paul's concept of principalities and powers was. (I have discussed the relation of *stoicheia* and religion to Paul's writing on principalities and powers in Mark D. Baker, "Responding to the Powers: Learning From Paul and Jesus" [M.A. thesis, New College for Advanced Christian Studies, Berkeley, 1990].) I will include Ellul's definition of the powers because it captures well what I am pointing to by calling religion a power. The argument of this book, however, does not depend on one accepting this definition. I focus more on how people experience religion, that it does enslave, rather than attempting to explain what constitutes religion in a cosmological sense. "[The powers] correspond to authentic, if spiritual, realities which are independent of man's decision and inclination and whose force does not reside in the man who constitutes them. . . . The powers do not act simply from outside after the manner of Gnostic destiny. . . . They are characterized by their relation to the concrete world of man. . . . The powers seem to be able to transform a natural, social, intellectual, or economic reality into a force which man has no ability either to resist or control" (Jacques Ellul, *The Ethics of Freedom* [Grand Rapids, Mich.: Eerdmans, 1976], p. 152).

[23]Compare Romans 7 and sin's "seizing" the law.

[24]Juan Luis Segundo, *Jesus of Nazareth Yesterday and Today*, vol. 3, *The Humanist Christology of Paul* (Maryknoll, N.Y.: Orbis, 1986), pp. 25-26. Segundo offers a Pauline study that presents the contrast between religion and faith as a major theme. In that sense, his work is very similar to mine. Segundo defines and describes *religion* close to the way I do in this book. His humanist description of faith, however, differs significantly from my description of faith and the gospel.

[25]John Barclay, *Obeying the Truth: A Study of Paul's Ethics in Galatians* (Edinburgh: T & T Clark, 1988), p. 71; see also p. 106.

[26]Other biblical scholars also point to insecurity as driving the Galatians' turn away from the gospel: "The Galatians had been given the 'Spirit' and 'Freedom.' . . . There was no law to tell them what was right or wrong. There were no more rituals to correct transgressions. Under these circumstances, their daily life came to be a dance on a tightrope! . . . [It] was quite understandable that the Galatians more or less decided to accept the recommendations of Paul's opponents, to have themselves circumcised, to become conscientious observers of the Torah and thereby 'heirs' of the security that this included" (H. D. Betz, *Galatians*, Hermeneia [Philadelphia: Fortress, 1979], p. 9). Gerhard Ebeling writes, "Liberation of the Gentile Galatians from bondage to the elemental spirits of the universe brought a deep sense of relief, but it could also bring a no less deep sense of insecurity as to where to find a firm anchor for life, in the face of such totally unaccustomed freedom" (Gerhard Ebeling, *The Truth of the Gospel: An Exposition of Galatians* [Philadelphia: Fortress, 1985], p. 251).

[27]Betz, *Galatians*, p. 3; Helmut Koester, *History, Culture and Religion of the Hellenistic Age*, Introduction to the New Testament 1 (Philadelphia: Fortress, 1982); Tamez, *Amnesty of Grace*, pp. 76, 186.

[28]The reconstruction of the background of Galatians is admittedly uncertain. J. Ross Wagner has pointed out to me that besides the psychological pressure on individuals described in this section, there was very likely corporate pressure as well. "It was a disadvantage for the church to seem to be a 'new' religion in a culture that valued antiquity. The Christian claim to be the heir of Jewish tradition was put in doubt by continuing opposition between church and synagogue. In addition, the relatively large number of Gentiles may have made the church less appealing to potential Jewish adherents. It is possible that Paul's opponents wanted Gentiles to become full proselytes by undergoing circumcision in order not to impede the on-going mission to Jews" (J. Ross Wagner, letter to the author, spring 1996). This observation further supports the basic thesis of this chapter that communal concerns drove Paul's writing this letter. For further information on this, see Paula Fredriksen, *From Jesus to Christ* (New Haven: Yale University Press, 1988), pp. 168-70.

[29]Rodney Clapp, *A Peculiar People: The Church as Culture in a Post-Christian Society* (Downers Grove, Ill.: InterVarsity Press, 1996), p. 107.

[30]Joel B. Green, *How to Read the Gospels and Acts* (Downers Grove, Ill.: InterVarsity Press, 1987), p. 49.

[31]For example, Matthew 8:11; 22:1-4; 23:23-26; 25:1-13; Mark 7:1-23; 12:39; 14:3-9; Luke 7:36-50; 10:38-42; 11:37-52; 12:35-38; 14:1-24; 15; 17:7-10; 19:1-10; 22:14-38.

[32]The Pharisees sought to tithe all foods and would not eat at the home of someone untrustworthy in regard to payment of tithes or preparation of foods. Pharisees could host non-Pharisees if they gave the non-Pharisee clean garments upon entering the house and if the guest was not someone whose presence alone might defile the house (Marcus J. Borg, *Conflict, Holiness and Politics in the Teachings of Jesus* [New York: Edwin Mellen, 1984], pp. 80-81; James D. G. Dunn, *Jesus, Paul and the Law: Studies in Mark and Galatians* [London: SPCK, 1990], p. 139). See also Martin Hengel and Roland Deines, "E. P. Sanders's 'Common Judaism,' Jesus, and the Pharisees: A Review Article," *Journal of Theological Studies* 46 (1995): 1-70 (especially pp. 41-51).

[33]Marcus J. Borg, *Jesus: A New Vision* (San Francisco: Harper & Row, 1987), p. 89.

[34]Of course, from the short description in Galatians 2 we do not know exactly what the

people from James considered problematic in Peter's actions. It could have been the food he ate with the Gentiles, just the fact that he ate with Gentiles, perhaps they had taken up a Gentile way of life in other ways or something in between. (See E. P. Sanders, "Jewish Association with Gentiles and Galatians 2:11-14," in *The Conversation Continues: Studies in Paul and John*, eds. Robert T. Fortna and Beverly Roberts Gaventa [Nashville: Abingdon, 1990], pp. 170-88; and Betz, *Galatians*, p. 104.) Philip F. Esler speculates that the Christian Eucharistic practice of sharing one cup and one loaf of bread is what made this table fellowship so controversial since, although some Jews allowed for mixed table-fellowship, they only did so on the condition that "one did not eat their meat or drink their wine" (*First Christians*, pp. 66-68). What is significant at this point, and apparently for Paul also, is not the details, but the fact of the separation based on religious rules.

[35]McKnight, *Galatians*, p. 25.

[36]Peter's position was defended in the *Kerygmata Petrou* (see Betz, *Galatians*, p. 104). Luke avoids it, but does admit that Paul and Barnabas split up (Acts 15:36-39).

[37]Charles B. Cousar, *Galatians* (Atlanta: John Knox Press, 1982), p. 47.

[38]This is a paraphrase of Hansen (*Galatians*, p. 68). I have placed "religion" as the central issue. Others describe it differently. John Barclay, for instance, writes:

> Paul opposes "the works of the law" in Galatians because they represent imposing a Jewish life-style ("living like a Jew" 2:14ff.) on his Gentile converts. The problem here is not legalism (in the sense of earning merit before God) but cultural imperialism—regarding Jewish identity and Jewish customs as the essential tokens of membership in the people of God. . . . God's saving activity is envisaged in racial and cultural terms. (Barclay, *Obeying the Truth*, p. 240)

This cultural imperialism, however, cannot be separated from religion. As Scot McKnight observes, "this cultural imperialism had become enmeshed in a religious system" (McKnight, *Galatians*, p. 25).

In the context of Las Mesetas and North American evangelicalism, it is helpful to see religion as a central issue Paul addresses, and that is why I stress it. In different contexts, people may choose to emphasize other factors. I still, however, want to push others, even if they emphasize another factor, to reflect more about religion as defined by Ellul or Segundo in relation to the problem in Galatia.

N. T. Wright's use of the idea of "badges" demonstrates the problem of not taking the deeper universal religious problem into account. Wright considers racial origin, circumcision and dietary customs as badges that demarcate covenant membership. This is a helpful description of what Paul is reacting against. Wright correctly portrays the Christian covenant community as more inclusive and writes that "for the Christian covenant membership is defined by Christ" (N. T. Wright, "Putting Paul Together Again: Toward a Synthesis of Pauline Theology," in *Pauline Theology: Toward a New Synthesis*, vol.1, ed. Jouette Bassler [Minneapolis: Fortress, 1991], p. 202). His mistake is picturing Paul saying that Christians have new badges. Wright states that Christians have given up "the false badges of covenant membership, . . . their only present badge being their faith" (Wright, "Putting Paul Together Again," p. 205). Their new badge is "believing *these things* (one God; one Lord; Jesus is Lord; God raised him from the dead; etc.)" (Wright, "Putting Paul Together Again," p. 202). Why talk about Christians having badges? Badges provide just what the religious part of us craves—something the individual can display to show he or she belongs. I recognize that Wright sees "faith" as very different from the "false badges of the covenant," but the fact that he gives such a prominent role to human faith (and believing "these things") demonstrates that he does not fully appreciate religion's capability to turn faith itself into a work, to use beliefs ("correct doctrine") as a religious boundary line fraught with the same potential for self-righteousness and division as the false badge of the covenant. To have linked the word *badge* with having a seat at the one united table of Christian fellowship demonstrates a failure to have understood the power of religion and hence the depth of the problem Paul confronted (Wright, "Putting Paul Together Again," pp. 201-7).

[39]Cousar, *Galatians*, p. 50.

Chapter 7: Justification by Faith

[1]See Krister Stendahl, *Paul Among Jews and Gentiles* (Philadelphia: Fortress, 1976), p. 12. Stendahl places the original "blame" for leading us to misunderstand Paul with Augustine (pp. 16-17).

[2]*Dios habla hoy: La Biblia—versión popular,* 2nd ed. (New York: American Bible Society, 1983). This translation is equivalent to Today's English Version Bible. It is approved by the Roman Catholic Church, and Catholic translators collaborated in the project, so this is not necessarily only a Protestant problem. My focus, however, is on the evangelical community.

[3]See 2:16a-b, 21; 3:8, 11, 21, 24; 5:4, 5.

[4]Except in the verb form, since *righteous* does not have one.

[5]Three English translations (KJV, NIV, NRSV) always translate the verb with a form of "justify." The other five uses of *dikai* words in Galatians are almost all translated with forms of "righteousness" (2:21; 3:6, 11, 21; 5:5). The New International Version uses "righteous" or "righteousness" in all five; the King James Version uses "just" in 3:11 and "righteousness" in the other four; the New Revised Standard Version uses "justification" in 2:21 and "righteous" or "righteousness" in the other four.

[6]In this section I lean heavily on an excellent article on "Justification" by Richard B. Hays in the *Anchor Bible Dictionary,* ed. David N. Freedman (New York: Doubleday, 1992), 3:1129-33.

[7]Hays, "Justification," p. 1132. Hays offers this description of the traditional position, but critiques this position in the article.

[8]N. T. Wright, "Justification: The Biblical Basis," in *The Great Acquittal,* ed. Gavin Reid (London: Collins, 1980), p. 36.

[9]John Driver, *Understanding the Atonement for the Mission of the Church* (Scottdale, Penn.: Herald Press, 1986) p. 32.

[10]See Hays, "Justification," p. 1129. The Qumran literature provides an excellent example of an acknowledged sinner who sees God's justice/righteousness as a basis for hope. The ease with which the word *righteousness* can be replaced by the phrase, "God's faithfulness to his covenant promise," demonstrates the relational understanding the author had of the word *righteousness*.

As for me, my judgment (*mispati*) is with God. In his hand are the perfection of my way and the uprightness of my heart. He will wipe out my transgression through his righteousness (*sidqotaw*). . . . As for me, if I stumble, the mercies of God shall be my eternal salvation. If I stagger because of the sin of flesh, my judgment (*mispati*) shall be by the righteousness of God (*sidqat el*) which endures for ever. (IQS 11:2-3, 12)

[11]Hays, "Justification," p. 1131; Dunn states that Paul's talk of justice/righteousness "derives directly from the Old Testament, as his two most famous OT quotations illustrate (3:6—Gen 15:6; 3:11—Hab 2:4)" (James D. G. Dunn, *The Theology of Paul's Letter to the Galatians* [Cambridge: Cambridge University Press, 1993], p. 76).

[12]N. T. Wright, "Putting Paul Together Again: Toward a Synthesis of Pauline Theology," in *Pauline Theology: Toward a New Synthesis* vol. 1, ed. Jouette Bassler (Minneapolis: Fortress, 1991), p. 201.

[13]Hays, "Justification," pp. 1131-32.

[14]Stendahl, *Paul Among Jews,* p. 40.

[15]Wright, "Justification: The Biblical Basis," p. 22. Other examples are Markus Barth, "Jews and Gentiles: The Social Character of Justification in Paul," *Journal of Ecumenical Studies* 5 (1968): 245-46; Charles B. Cousar, *Galatians* (Atlanta: John Knox Press, 1982), p. 58; Nils A. Dahl, *Studies in Paul* (Minneapolis: Augsburg, 1977), p. 111; and James D. G. Dunn and Alan M. Suggate, *The Justice of God: A Fresh Look at the Old Doctrine of Justification by Faith* (Grand Rapids, Mich.: Eerdmans. 1993), p. 25.

[16]Dahl, *Studies in Paul,* p. 110.

[17]Markus Barth, "Jews and Gentiles," p. 259. Gerald Borchert agrees: "Christians, whether they are monastics, pietists or evangelical individualists, who focus their attention concerning salvation and experience with God solely on individual accountability with God, will certainly fail to comprehend the full nature of Paul's understanding of living with the God who sent Jesus. Paul could not think of relationship with Christ apart from the community" (Gerald L. Borchert, "A Key to Pauline Thinking—Galatians 3:23-29: Faith and the New Humanity," *Review and Expositor* 91 [1994]: 148).

[18]Dunn argues that for many Jews, "the practice of the law, the works of the law, which most clearly maintained covenant distinctiveness from other peoples in the practicalities of daily life were those which governed table-fellowship" (Dunn, *Theology,* p. 78). This makes a very strong link between the preceding incident at Antioch and the phrase "works of the law."

[19]G. Walter Hansen, *Galatians,* IVP New Testament Commentary (Downers Grove, Ill.: InterVarsity Press, 1994), p. 69. See also John Barclay, *Obeying the Truth: A Study of Paul's Ethics in Galatians* (Edinburgh: T & T Clark, 1988), p. 82; James D. G. Dunn, *A Commentary on the Epistle to the Galatians* (London: A. C. Black, 1993), pp. 134-38; James D. G. Dunn, *Jesus, Paul and the Law: Studies in Mark and Galatians* (London: SPCK, 1990), pp. 194-95; Dunn, *Theology,* pp. 77-79; Richard Longenecker, *Galatians,* Word Biblical Commentary (Dallas: Word, 1990), p. 86.

[20]As I discussed in chapter six, Jewish teaching was not legalistic. It did not teach that Jews earned a place within the covenant community by these practices. Rather the practices identified them as what they were by God's action—the people of God. Longenecker, however, argues that when "foisted on Gentile Christians" they became legalistic (*Galatians,* p. 86).

[21]Barth, "Jews and Gentiles," p. 251.

[22]For example, Markus Barth, "The Faith of the Messiah," *Heythrop Journal* 10 (1969): 363-70; William Dalton, *Galatians Without Tears* (Collegeville, Minn.: Liturgical Press, 1992), pp. 41-46; Richard B. Hays, *The Faith of Jesus Christ: An Investigation of the Narrative Substructure of Gal. 3:1—4:11,* Society of Biblical Literature Dissertation Series 56 (Chico, Calif.: Scholars Press, 1983), pp. 139-91; Richard B. Hays, "Jesus' Faith and

Ours: A Rereading of Galatians 3," in *Conflict and Context: Hermeneutics in the Americas,* ed. Mark Lau Branson and C. René Padilla (Grand Rapids, Mich.: Eerdmans, 1986), pp. 257-80; Richard B. Hays, "*Pistis* and Pauline Christology," *Society of Biblical Literature Seminar Papers* (1991): 714-29; George Howard, "On the Faith of Christ," *Harvard Theological Review* 60 (1967): 459-84; Luke T. Johnson, "Romans 3:21-26 and the Faith of Jesus," *Catholic Biblical Quarterly* 44 (1982): 77-90; Longenecker, *Galatians,* pp. 87-88, 93-94, 145. Those arguing for the objective genitive include F. F. Bruce, *The Epistle to the Galatians: A Commentary on the Greek Text,* NIGTC (Grand Rapids, Mich.: Eerdmans, 1982), pp. 138-39; James D. G. Dunn, "Once More *Pistis Christou*," *SBL Seminar Papers* (1991): 730-44; Ronald Y. K. Fung, *The Epistle to the Galatians* (Grand Rapids, Mich.: Eerdmans, 1988), pp. 114-15. Rather than enter into the details of the argument for one translation or the other, I will simply refer the reader to the works cited in this footnote.

[23]At the conference on hermeneutics in the Americas where Richard Hays presented his paper "Jesus' Faith and Ours," Moisés Silva, who favors the objective genitive, critiqued Hays's position. Hays responded and then concluded, "In the end, Dr. Silva and I agree that the expression *pistis Iēsou Christou* is ambiguous, that its ambiguity must be resolved by appealing to broader contextual considerations, and that no irrefutable resolution of the ambiguity is possible on either side" (Richard Hays, "Postscript: Further Reflections on Galatians 3," in *Conflict and Context: Hermeneutics in the Americas,* eds. Mark Lau Branson and C. René Padilla [Grand Rapids, Mich.: Eerdmans, 1986], p. 278).

[24]Evidence for this is the way the opposing camps look at the same piece of information and state that it clearly demonstrates theirs is the correct translation. For instance, both sides agree that the middle phrase in 2:16 refers to human faith or trust in Christ Jesus. The objective genitive camp, however, takes this as proof that the first phrase is also "faith in." They say Paul would not offer contradictory statements in the same verse (Fung, *Epistle to the Galatians,* p. 115; Scot McKnight, *Galatians,* NIV Application Commentary [Grand Rapids, Mich.: Zondervan, 1995], p. 122). The other camp states it would be redundant for Paul to repeat the same thing three times in one verse. Therefore "faith of" is the most natural reading of the first and third uses of *pistis* in this verse. In this way, Paul sets "out both the objective and the subjective bases for the Christian life" (Longenecker, *Galatians,* p. 88; see also Hays, "Jesus' Faith and Ours," p. 262; Markus Barth, "The Kerygma of Galatians," *Interpretation* 21 (April 1967): 144-45).

[25]Karl Barth, *The Church Dogmatics* 4.1 (Edinburgh: T & T Clark, 1956): 615-16. William Law states, "Suppose one man were to rely on his own faith and another on his own works, then the faith of the one and the works of the other are equally the same worthless filthy rags" (quoted in Hays, *Faith of Jesus Christ,* p. 139). See also Dalton, *Galatians Without Tears,* pp. 43, 45; Hays, "Jesus' Faith and Ours," p. 267; Hays, "Justification," p. 1131.

[26]Hays, "Justification," p. 1131.

[27]In this regard it is interesting that Silva critiqued Hays's characterization of "justifying faith" as a "work" by stating that was not the Reformation's understanding of faith. For them, faith was a relinquishment of effort to obtain justification. Hays responded that his attack is not directed against the Reformers, "but against their historical successors, particularly twentieth-century evangelicals, among whom this tendency [to turn faith into a work] is epidemic" (Hays, "Postscript," p. 278). Silva does exactly what I critiqued in chapter six. He appeals to official teaching. Hays, however, points to what is lived out.

[28]Hays, *"Pistis,"* pp. 715-16.

[29]Hays, "Jesus' Faith and Ours," p. 263. Longenecker offers a very similar translation (*Galatians,* p. 81). "When the genitive is taken as subjective, the phrase is variously interpreted as meaning 'Christ's faith' (in God), or 'Christ's faithfulness' (to God), or God's faithfulness revealed in Christ" (Bruce, *Epistle to the Galatians,* p. 139). I prefer the meaning reflected in Hays's translation. It coheres well with the relational view of justification I have described above. The main point in the previous section, however, is that the subjective genitive places more emphasis on God's action. That is true of all three of the options Bruce lists. Also, in a sense, the three blend together. God proves to be a faithful covenant partner (just) by providing a means of justification (Christ's faithful obedience), and Jesus obeyed in faith, trusting God the Father.

[30]It is unclear where Paul's speech to Peter ends—clearly it has ended by 3:1. Whether Paul is reporting what he said to Peter, or speaking to the Galatians—reflecting on the incident with Peter—is not crucial. What is crucial is to recognize the link of these verses (2:15-21) to the Antioch incident. To make too big a division between 2:11-14 and 2:15-21 de-emphasizes this link. (For instance, Bruce starts a whole new chapter in his commentary at 2:15.)

[31]Barth, "Kerygma of Galatians," p. 142.

Chapter 8: New Creation: Freedom from Religion & Freedom for Community

[1]Jacques Ellul, "The Meaning of Freedom According to Saint Paul," in *Sources and Trajectories: Eight Early Articles by Jacques Ellul That Set the Stage,* translation and commentary by Marva J. Dawn (Grand Rapids, Mich.: Eerdmans, 1997), p. 119.

[2]J. Louis Martyn, "Events in Galatia: Modified Covenantal Nomism Versus God's Invasion of the Cosmos in the Singular Gospel," in *Pauline Theology,* vol. 1, ed. Jouette M. Bassler (Minneapolis: Fortress, 1991), p. 163.

[3]Ibid., 161; See also Pieter J. J. Botha, "Letter Writing and Oral Communication in Antiquity: Suggested Implications for the Interpretation of Paul's Letter to the Galatians," *Scriptura* 42 (1992): 21.

[4]The section titles and divisions of this chapter are not meant to present an "outline" of Galatians in the sense of giving the best breakdown of the structure and argument of the letter. Rather, I have divided the sections and titled them as I have to highlight the central themes of this book—religion and community.

[5]See 1:1, 11-12, 16; 2:6-7. Most commonly, it is assumed that Paul makes these statements to bolster his authority. That may be part of the reason. They also, however, clearly separate the gospel from human religion.

[6]See Michael Winger, "Tradition, Revelation and Gospel: A Study in Galatians," *Journal for the Study of the New Testament* 53 (1994): 65-66.

[7]Richard B. Hays, *Galatians,* New Interpreters Bible, vol. 11 (Nashville: Abingdon, forthcoming), p. 3.

[8]J. Louis Martyn, *Galatians,* Anchor Bible (New York: Doubleday, 1997), pp. 81, 90.

[9]Hays, *Galatians,* p. 3.

[10]H. D. Betz, *Galatians,* Hermeneia [Philadelphia: Fortress, 1979], p. 101.

[11]I am not attempting in two paragraphs to adequately explain a doctrine of sin. I have, however, tried to highlight two important points. The first is seeing that sin at root is a relational rather than an ontological problem. The second is to acknowledge that to describe the fundamental sin in terms of pride does not accurately describe everyone's experience and may actually serve to encourage or sacralize a diminished self, which

may be just as much a product of alienation as someone else's pride. For a helpful discussion of these issues see Carol Lakey Hess, *Caretakers of Our Common House* (Nashville: Abingdon, 1997), pp. 31-54. I have also found Margaret G. Alter's discussion of Adam and Eve very helpful in her *Resurrection Pyschology: An Understanding of Human Personality Based on the Life and Teachings of Jesus* (Chicago: Loyola University Press, 1994), pp. 1-18.

[12]I do not mean that Paul does not have clear ideas on what might be appropriate and inappropriate behavior. As will be discussed later, he has strong ethical concerns, but he does not discuss them or live them out in a religious way.

[13]For an in-depth study of this theme in Paul, see Charles B. Cousar, *A Theology of the Cross: The Death of Jesus in the Pauline Letters* (Minneapolis: Fortress, 1990).

[14]Two pieces where Luther explicitly uses the terms *theology of glory* and *theology of the cross*, and discusses them at some length are "Heidelberg Disputation" (April 1518) and "Explanations of the Ninety-Five Theses" (1518). English translations for both are in *Luther's Works*, vol. 31, ed. Jaroslav Pelikan and Helmut Lehmann (Philadelphia: Fortress, 1957). See also Walther von Loewenich, *Luther's Theology of the Cross* (Minneapolis: Augsburg, 1967); Alister E. McGrath, *Luther's Theology of the Cross: Martin Luther's Theological Breakthrough* (Oxford: Basil Blackwell, 1985); and Deanna Thompson, "Theological Proximity to the Cross: A Conversation Between Martin Luther and Feminist Theologians" (Ph.D. diss., Vanderbilt University, 1998).

[15]Martin Luther, *Galatians* 1535 (Gal. 1:3), (W, XL 77, 78)—this translation in Gerhard Ebeling, *Luther: An Introduction to His Thought* (Philadelphia: Fortress, 1972), p. 235. A different translation is in *Luther's Works*, vol. 26, pp. 29-31.

[16]In this sentence I have placed the emphasis on the gospel itself rather than the Galatians' response to it. It makes sense that Paul would de-emphasize the human role, as we have already seen in relation to 4:9, but many translations of *ex akoēs pisteos* (3:2, 5) do the opposite.

Akoē can mean either the act of hearing or that which is heard (report, message, proclamation), and *pistis* can mean either the act of believing or that which is believed (the faith). Richard Hays lays out the following four possible translations of this phrase in Richard B. Hays, *The Faith of Jesus Christ: An Investigation of the Narrative Substructure of Gal. 3:1-4:11*, Society for Biblical Literature Dissertation Series 56 (Chico, Calif.: Scholars Press, 1983), p. 143; see also Richard Longenecker, *Galatians*, Word Biblical Commentary (Dallas: Word, 1990), p. 102-3.

* if *akoē* means "hearing":
   a. (*pistis* = "believing") "by hearing with faith"
   b. (*pistis* = "the faith") "by hearing" 'the faith' " = "by hearing the gospel."
* if *akoē* means "message, proclamation":
   c. (*pistis* = "believing") "from the message that enables faith"
   d. (*pistis* = "the faith") "from the message of 'the faith' " = "the gospel-message."

All four translations have their advocates, but "a" ("by hearing with faith") has been most popular and reflects the general "Protestant" understanding of Paul's message. Those who opt for this translation use the parallel expressions of 3:2 to defend the translation. In essence then they see Paul expressing this thought: "You received the Spirit not because you did X (= performed works) but because you did Y (= heard and believed)" (Hays, *Faith of Jesus Christ*, p. 144). Is that the message of Galatians? Before returning to this question we will look at evidence favoring another translation.

Translators who choose "a" have, of course, made a decision about how to translate both words. To evaluate their translation we must ask questions about both words. First, *pistis*. Even within Galatians (1:23), *pistis* acts as direct object when Paul proclaimed the faith. (See also 3:23-26 and 6:10.) So, "the faith" or "the gospel" are arguably possible translations. On the other hand, the lack of a definite article weakens this possibility. Hays argues that "perhaps the truth of the matter is that Paul's compressed language will not answer all the questions that we would like to put to it and that he did not intend a clear distinction: *akoē* pisteos means simply 'the faith-message,' and the attempt to distinguish between 'the message that evokes faith' and 'the message of 'the faith' is our problem rather than Paul's" (*Faith of Jesus Christ*, p. 149).

The decision on how to translate *akoē* is more significant. There are strong arguments in favor of "message" and against the active "hearing." Paul uses the word elsewhere in both senses. Romans 10:16-17 is the usage that comes closest to the Galatian context. In Romans 10:16, *akoē* unambiguously means "message"; the usage in 10:17 is open to question, but since it is a comment on 10:16, the same translation would seem appropriate. A strong case cannot be built on Paul's other uses of *akoē*, but if anything they support the "message, proclamation" translation in Galatians.

Proponents of option "a" place much weight on the parallel structure of the verse. Options "c" or "d," however, fit this structure as well or better. " 'Works' do not stand in the same relation to 'Law' as does 'hearing' to 'faith.'. . . The truth of the matter is that the juxtaposed phrases must be taken as indivisible meaning-units: 'Did you receive the Spirit from x or from y?' . . . Betz's translation captures the proper sense of the matter by placing each phrase in quotation marks so that it becomes clear that each one is a catch phrase or slogan" (Hays, *Faith of Jesus Christ*, p. 147). "This only do I want to learn from you: did you receive the Spirit by 'works of [the] Law' or by [the] 'proclamation of [the] faith'? (Gal. 3:2) (Betz, *Galatians*, p. 128].

Finally, translating *akoē* as "message" or "proclamation" makes more sense both in relation to these specific verses and to Paul's previous contrast in Galatians between a message sent by God, not by humans. Rather than to say the Spirit comes not through one human activity ("works"), but another ("believing-hearing"), Paul desires to say the Spirit comes not through human action, but by God's acting through the message proclaimed. This is especially clear in 3:5 where God is placed as the actor. Paul's question, "Does God supply you with the Spirit and work miracles among you by your doing the works of the law?" sounds almost ridiculous. One would answer, "Of course not." In the same way to ask, "Does God supply you with the Spirit and work miracles among you by your believing what you heard?" should sound a little ridiculous. Since God is placed as the actor it makes more sense to ask, "Did God supply you with the Spirit and work miracles among you through the proclamation of the gospel?"

What Paul writes in 1 Thessalonians 1:4-5 offers an argument similar to Galatians 3:1-5. Paul offers the work of the Spirit as evidence of inclusion in both places. 1 Thessalonians 1:5 unambiguously describes the message of the gospel as the agent, coming to them in power (see also Rom 1:16). Therefore, it is not only conceivable, but probable, considering the general message of Galatians, that Paul meant to place the emphasis on God's acting through the proclamation of the gospel. In 3:2 and 5 *akoē* is best translated as "message" or "proclamation."

[17]Richard B. Hays, "*Pistis* and Pauline Christology," *Society of Biblical Literature Seminar Papers* (1991): 727; see also Richard B. Hays, "Jesus' Faith and Ours: A Rereading of Galatians 3," in *Conflict and Context: Hermeneutics in the Americas*, eds. Mark Lau Branson and C. René Padilla (Grand Rapids, Mich.: Eerdmans, 1986), pp.

262-63. Longenecker offers this translation of 3:22b: "so that the promise that is based on the faithfulness of Jesus Christ might be given to those who believe" (*Galatians*, p. 136). Note that here, as in 2:16, this translation still recognizes the significance of human belief or faith. In a similar way, Hays argues that we should understand the faith that came in 3:23 and 25 as an event—the coming of Christ. The fact that Paul does not explicitly say "the coming of Christ," just the faith that came, probably means he includes those of the faith who participate in Christ and his destiny (*Faith of Jesus Christ*, pp. 230-32).

[18]This is not to say that reflecting on our explanations of the atonement is unimportant. For an exploration of that theme in relation to the mission of the church, see Mark D. Baker and Joel B. Green, *The Scandal of the Cross* (Downers Grove, Ill.: InterVarsity Press, forthcoming); and John Driver, *Understanding the Atonement for the Mission of the Church* (Scottdale, Penn.: Herald Press, 1986). Irenaeus's recapitulation theory, which is closely linked with Romans 5, is one explanation (See Hays, *Faith of Jesus Christ*, p. 248) that coheres well with the participatory concept of being "in Christ" common in Galatians (*e.g.,* 2:4, 17; 3:26-29; 5:6). See Longenecker, *Galatians*, p. 85.

[19]In this sense, Martyn's emphasis on the apocalyptic essence of Paul's message is quite helpful in J. Louis Martyn, "Apocalyptic Antinomies in Paul's Letter to the Galatians," *New Testament Studies* 31 (1985): 410-24. See also Colossians 2:15.

[20]Luther, *Luther's Works*, vol. 26, p. 356.

[21]Beverly Roberts Gaventa contends that the central theological claim of Galatians is "that the gospel proclaims Jesus Christ crucified to be the inauguration of a new creation (Beverly Roberts Gaventa, "The Singularity of the Gospel: A Reading of Galatians" in *Pauline Theology*, vol. 1, ed. Jouette M. Bassler [Minneapolis: Fortress, 1991], p. 159).

[22]Paul clearly expects the new creation community to be different, and in that sense it is appropriate to discuss how it is different or has boundaries. Yet the inclusive nature of the community contrasts markedly with the boundaries of religious communities, which attempt what the gospel tears down. In reference to Jesus' redefinition of the world and listing of behaviors appropriate to this new community, such as loving enemies (Luke 6:32-35), Joel Green makes a similar observation about boundaries. He writes:

> One corollary of Jesus' message, then, is the construction of a boundary, the delineation of behavior characteristic of those within the community. This is an important observation, since one of the distinguishing marks of his ethic is a worldview that advocates love of enemies. But as a practice, it would appear that love of enemies is designed to mitigate social tensions that, if habitual, would jeopardize the identity of any group. How can this community be distinguished by a practice that dissolves any such distinctions? . . . Jesus calls on his followers to form a community the boundaries of which are porous and whose primary emblematic behavior is its refusal to treat others . . . as though they were enemies. (Joel B. Green, *The Gospel of Luke*, New International Commentary on the New Testament [Grand Rapids, Mich.: Eerdmans, 1997], p. 270)

[23]Clapp, *A Peculiar People*, p. 100.

Chapter 9: New Creation: An Ethic of Freedom for Christian Community
[1]John Barclay, *Obeying the Truth: A Study of Paul's Ethics in Galatians* (Edinburgh: T & T Clark, 1988), p. 115; Scot McKnight, *Galatians*, The NIV Application Commentary

(Grand Rapids, Mich.: Zondervan, 1995), p. 265. I will discuss the term *flesh* later in this section.

[2]Ellul, "Meaning of Freedom," pp. 122-3.

[3]Ibid., p. 120.

[4]C. Norman Kraus, interview by the author at Associated Mennonite Biblical Seminary, Elkhart, Ind., October 28, 1994.

[5]Some have, in fact, found this section so different from the rest of Galatians that they have speculated that Paul was dealing with two different problems in one letter. For examples, see Barclay, *Obeying the Truth*, pp. 9-16. Although there is a notable shift toward ethical instruction in these verses, that does not mean that Paul has turned to a new topic. John Barclay argues that we will fail to grasp the full significance of these verses "if we do not see [them] in the context of Paul's debate with the Galatians. These verses are not an independent or dispassionate account of Christian ethics tacked on to the end of an argumentative letter, but a continuation and completion of the argument" (*Obeying the Truth*, p. 143). Although a traditional individualistic reading of justification by faith would provide little continuity with this section, there is great continuity between this section and the reading of justification by Christ's faithfulness used in this book. An individualistic understanding of justification that focuses on one individual's position in God's legal ledger does not naturally lead to a discussion about how to live together as a community. If, however, we understand justification as God bringing people together, than it would be quite appropriate to discuss how to live together. Paul's indicative statement is that, in Jesus Christ, God has included the Galatians in the one people of God. Paul now offers the imperative challenge to live in unity as the one people of God.

[6]Markus Barth, *Ephesians*, Anchor Bible (Garden City, N.Y.: Doubleday, 1974), p. 453. See also Barclay, *Obeying the Truth*, pp. 225-27.

[7]Scholars have interpreted the phrase "the law of Christ" in a number of ways (see Richard Hays, "Christology and Ethics in Galatians: The Law of Christ," *Catholic Biblical Quarterly* 49 [1987]: 273-76). What we can say clearly is that to bear one another's burdens relates centrally to the law of Christ. Based on his reading of Galatians, Hays argues that the law of Christ "is a formulation coined (or employed) by Paul to refer to [the] paradigmatic self-giving of Jesus Christ" (Hays, "Christology and Ethics," p. 275). In Galatians 1:3-4, Paul speaks of "the Lord Jesus Christ, who gave himself for our sins to set us free from the present evil age, according to the will of our God and Father." The theme of Christ's redemptive self-giving in obedience to God's will appears again in 2:20. The locus of this giving was his death on the cross (2:21). The meaning and result of Christ's death are further explicated in 3:13-14 and 4:4-7. Hays concludes, "Even if Galatians were the only source for our knowledge of Paul's Christology, we would know that Paul understood Jesus Christ as God's Son who simultaneously expressed obedience to God and love for humankind through surrendering himself to a death which somehow was vicariously efficacious to set others free" (Hays, "Christology and Ethics," p. 277).

[8]We see evidence of this type of regulations in the tradition that developed around Jewish law. For instance, they developed very specific rules about what constituted work on the sabbath.

[9]Barclay, *Obeying the Truth*, p. 230.

[10]Ellul, "Meaning of Freedom," p. 120.

[11]Barclay, *Obeying the Truth*, p. 213. Cousar writes: "The Spirit and the flesh in this context

are not components of human nature but two realities on which individuals can base their existence, two directions toward which they can move. . . . What Paul means by the flesh needs a certain bit of translation for contemporary Christians. He is not saying that material things are inherently evil, nor is he implying that human feelings, physical desires, or sensual pleasures are themselves to be avoided or suppressed. What makes the flesh so destructive is that it can become the norm by which people's lives are lived. This world, with its measures of success and its rewards for hard work, absorbs all their interests and demands their full attention. There is no openness to God's activity, to the presence of the Spirit, to the life of the new age" (Charles B. Cousar, *Galatians* [Atlanta: John Knox Press, 1982], pp. 137-38).

[12]See also 4:29.

[13]In reviewing a book by James D. G. Dunn, Richard Hays notes that "Dunn's methodological suggestion—that the crucial theological issues are flagged in the letter's opening and closing framework—yields important insights." But Hays points out that Dunn did not follow his own procedure strictly enough. "'Faith' is not mentioned as a theme in the introduction or conclusion." Yet Dunn emphasizes the importance of the human "faith in" Jesus. (Richard B. Hays, review of James D. G. Dunn, *The Theology of Paul's Letter to the Galatians*, in *Journal of Biblical Literature* 114, no. 4 [1995]: 748.)

[14]In addition to Gal 6:12-13, see 1:10 and 5:26.

Chapter 10: Responding to Religion Today

[1]Dwight Ozard, "Unashamed (Part One): Reclaiming the Evangel from American Evangelicals," *Prism* (November/December 1996): 5.

[2]Robert A. Hill, "What a Friend We Have in Paul," Sermon at Asbury First United Methodist Church, Rochester, N.Y., Oct. 12, 1997.

[3]I hardly claim to have an exhaustive list, but I have found it helpful to read sermons by Karl Barth, Robert Hill and Rowan Williams and to listen to tapes of Earl Palmer's sermons (Karl Barth, *Call For God* [New York: Harper & Row, 1965] and *Deliverance to the Captives* [New York: Harper & Row, 1978]; Rowan Williams, *A Ray of Darkness: Sermons and Reflections* [Boston: Cowley, 1995]; Robert Hill's sermons are available from Asbury First United Methodist Church, 1050 East Avenue, Rochester, N.Y. 14607; tapes of Earl Palmer's sermons are available from University Presbyterian Church, 4540 15th Ave. NE, Seattle, WA 98105).

[4]Vernard Eller, *The Promise: Ethics in the Kingdom of God* (Garden City, N.Y.: Doubleday, 1970); and *The Simple Life: The Christian Stance Toward Possessions* (Grand Rapids, Mich.: Eerdmans, 1972); Jacques Ellul, *The Ethics of Freedom* (Grand Rapids, Mich.: Eerdmans, 1976) and *To Will and To Do* (Philadelphia: Pilgrim, 1969); and Christos Yannaras, *The Freedom of Morality* (Crestwood, N.Y.: St. Vladimir's Seminary Press, 1984).

[5]David Gill, comment during "Jacques Ellul Discussion Group," November 2, 1987, New College Berkeley.

[6]I do not mean to deny that prayer and reading the Bible, or the lack of doing that, will influence our lives. But I maintain that for many the attitude I describe goes beyond the fruit of the activity itself and sees devotions as part of a religious-bargaining relationship.

Chapter 11: Individuals & New-Creation Community

[1]Frederick Herzog, *Liberation Theology: Liberation in the Light of the Fourth Gospel* (New York: Seabury Press, 1972), p. 79.

[2]Roberta Bondi, "Becoming Bearers of Reconciliation," *Weavings* 5, no. 1 (1990): 9-10.
[3]Besides the people of Amor Fe y Vida, the other key factor in my new interpretation of Galatians was Richard Hays. While preparing for leading the study on Galatians at Amor Fe y Vida Church in 1992, I read an essay by Hays that first led me to question the traditional reading of Galatians that I was accustomed to (Richard B. Hays, "Jesus' Faith and Ours: A Rereading of Galatians 3," in *Conflict and Context: Hermeneutics in the Americas*, eds. Mark Lau Branson and C. René Padilla [Grand Rapids, Mich.: Eerdmans, 1986], pp. 257-80). While reading the essay I began to think of a number of significant implications of Hays's approach in relation to the problems I saw in Las Mesetas. Less than a year later, I had the opportunity to study with Hays at Duke University. After having further developed my thinking on Galatians, I returned to Honduras in 1993 and worked through Galatians again with the people of Amor Fe y Vida. I then returned to Duke and did further work in Galatians.